FINDING

Your Voice

IN THE PSALMS

FINDING *Your Voice* IN THE PSALMS

AN INVITATION TO HONEST PRAYER

ELIZABETH J. CANHAM

UPPER ROOM BOOKS®
NASHVILLE

Front Cover Design: Nancy Terzian/BuckinghorseDesign.com
Back Cover and Interior Design: Nelson Kane

Library of Congress Cataloging-in-Publication Data
Canham, Elizabeth, 1939–
    Finding your voice in the Psalms : an invitation to honest prayer / by Elizabeth J. Canham.
    p. cm.
    ISBN 978-0-8358-1195-8 (print) — ISBN 978-0-8358-1196-5 (mobi) —
    ISBN 978-0-8358-1197-2 (epub)
    1. Bible. O.T. Psalms — Devotional literature. I. Title.
    BS1430.54.C36 2013
    242'.5—dc23

                                        2012024365

Printed in the United States of America

I dedicate this book to all seekers after truth,
especially the people of Calvary Episcopal Church
in Fletcher, North Carolina,
who taught me so much through our study together of the psalms.

CONTENTS ∿

PREFACE ∾

G OD'S PEOPLE have been praying the Psalms for many centuries.
There is much wisdom that resonates deep within us in these
prayers of our forbears, even though some of the images may need
reinterpretation in our present age. The Christian church adopted
the Hebrew Psalter early in its life. Saint John Chrysostom wrote in
the fourth century CE that the singing of psalms is "first, midst and
last" in Christian worship. Liturgical churches continue to include the
Psalter in the daily office, Eucharist, and at other times the people of
God gather.

The Psalms give voice to the wide range of human emotions that
arise in everyday experience. Jewish and Christian worshipers derive
comfort, hope, encouragement, and joy from these ancient prayers
but also find a way to cry out through them in anger, fear, and doubt
over the power and goodness of God. Individuals unable to worship
corporately also find that the psalms speak to their needs. The well-
known Twenty-third Psalm has brought comfort to countless people
who are sick and dying.

During the years I lived and worked in a Benedictine monastery
we chanted numerous psalms each day. At times I struggled to sing
the intricate chants we practiced each week in choir, but rarely did
I leave the chapel without a word or phrase that accompanied me
throughout the day. Sometimes the theme of a psalm did not resonate
with my personal experience. On a day when I was feeling blessed
and aware of the Holy One, we would sing a psalm of distress or

anger at God; but I could allow the psalm to become an offering of intercession for any who were suffering and afraid. Sometimes the words were transformative, leading me to spend time with my journal and kindling prayerful desire to be more fully alive to grace. Other times—especially during the predawn office—I was sleepy and inattentive or bored. But the community carried me. The Psalms are prayers that address the vicissitudes of life experienced by all God's people. I came to love these prayers as never before.

In this book I share my delight in the Psalms. I write for all heart-hungry people of God who must pray in the midst of very busy lives. Chapter 1 describes a model for praying with the psalms and a process for creating new psalms, inspired by scriptural psalms, that speak to current personal and communal experience. Each subsequent chapter closes with guidance for writing a psalm related to that chapter's theme. Those who wish to join others in reflection will find a model for using this book in a group context.

ELIZABETH J. CANHAM

INTRODUCTION ～

E ACH MORNING at 5:20 the bell begins to ring, calling the community to prayer. One by one monks appear and make their way
over the dew-soaked grass to take their place in the church. One or
two visitors join the community members to begin the morning with
recitation of psalms, scripture reading, and prayers. At all other ser-
vices we chant the Psalms, but in the morning, as we emerge from
sleep, we say them together. Singing in tune is a bit too challenging
so early in the day. Depending on the time of year, the morning worship might begin in darkness. The church is lit with candles, and the
lingering fragrance of incense from Sunday's Eucharist wafts in the
air. There is a sense of freshness, new beginnings, and preparation to
live the coming day consciously with God. It is a gift to be here, to
plunge into the ancient prayers of the Hebrew people and to discover
their blessing for the day.

I fell in love with the Psalms when I moved to Holy Savior Priory
in the South Carolina Lowcountry in 1985. During the four previous
years I had lived in New York City and had come to know many of
the Benedictine (Episcopal) brothers in the Order of the Holy Cross
at their monastery in West Park, New York. Whenever I could take a
break from parish ministry, I would board the train for the eighty-mile
journey beside the Hudson River to Poughkeepsie. I also introduced
members of my parish to the community by offering retreats at the
monastery. Most of the members of Saint Bartholomew's Episcopal
Church in Manhattan had never encountered monks and were unaware

that religious orders existed within the Episcopal Church. They were deeply moved by the silence, chanting, and beauty of worship. When the monk who had been my spiritual director was appointed prior to serve a daughter house in South Carolina, I was invited to become a monastic oblate and to serve as program director there. For the next five years I lived with the community—sharing the work, worship, and daily life, including weekly choir practice where we learned the intricate chants that lent such beauty to the singing of the Psalms.

Monastic chant of the Psalms appeals to many today who find the gentle, rhythmic singing a soothing introduction to meditation. Recordings of chant sell in great quantities, and monasteries are receiving a record number of guests looking for a different pace of life. The Psalms draw people in because they represent prayer uttered from the whole range of human experience. Even those of us who do not participate in community singing of the Psalter can relate to the down-to-earth cries of God's people in these ancient songs. Through the Psalms God's people have wept together, celebrated victory, danced, made music, lamented, and found hope in Yahweh. Jewish and Christian people alike have cherished the Psalter as a means of praying with integrity. The Psalms of the Hebrew scriptures quickly acquired a fixed place in the church, which chanted the entire Psalter weekly. Over the centuries our liturgies have reduced the number of psalms in worship, but the practice of reciting the whole Psalter on a regular basis has been preserved within monastic communities.

I discovered at the monastery that worship beginning in silence and punctuated by many pauses allows time for deeper connection with the One to whom we pray. All too often in church the service moves so quickly that it is difficult to be attentive to or even to hear what God may be trying to say to us. In my own Anglican tradition, the Book of Common Prayer repeatedly notes that after a reading or sermon "silence may be kept," but rarely do we honor those pauses. Clergy sometimes fear that silence will make the congregation grow anxious. We seldom take time for stillness in our culture. Monastic life is countercultural in that it punctuates each day with periods of silence. Monastics are no less busy than the rest of us; the telephone rings, guests arrive at the door, the grass needs to be mowed, food must be prepared—but when they (and we) attend to tasks from a place of stillness, it enhances the quality of Presence. The Psalms introduce a rhythm that reminds me of the ocean as wave upon wave reaches the shore, sometimes gently, sometimes with crashing vigor, but always with regularity. As I sat each day with the monks and learned to pause at the end of each line of a psalm—alien to my usual way of reading—I began to let the Psalms pray me. Today, with no community to assist my praying, I find that if I continue to practice the frequent pauses, I am more able to "hear" what God is saying through these ancient prayers.

ONE

Developing Honest Prayer

THE PSALMS CAN HELP US to pray with body, mind, and spirit. The beauty and wonder of creation is writ large in the Psalms; so is encouragement to celebrate God's praise through movement, dance, body prayer, and music. The following model will help us to pray the Psalms.

Praying with the Psalms

1. Begin with prayer.
Before reading the psalm (or any other portion of scripture) take time to be still in God's presence and ask the Holy Spirit to guide your reading and reflection. It may be helpful to repeat a psalm phrase several times and to breathe deeply with intention to listen. Two phrases I find useful are these: "For God alone my soul waits in silence" (Ps. 62:1) and "'Be still, and know that I am God!'" (Ps. 46:10).

2. Read slowly.
Today we are accustomed to skimming the newspaper or other written material because there is so much of it. This is not how literate people in the ancient world read. They read not only with their eyes but also

with their lips, and each word was spoken carefully. One model for reading scripture that keeps us focused on the text is the Benedictine practice of *lectio divina*:

After initial silence follow these steps:

Lectio (Reading). Read the psalm or a portion of it slowly (out loud if it will not disturb anyone), and then reflect on the text to see if a word or phrase "pops up."

Ruminatio (Meditation). Read a second time and "chew" (ruminate) on the words. Ask yourself, "How does this touch my life today?"

Oratio (Response). Read once more, allowing yourself to reflect more deeply as you listen for God's word to you. Your response to God emerges from that listening. You allow God to begin the conversation and *oratio* (response) follows.

Contemplatio (Contemplation). The purpose of *lectio divina* is to bring you to a place of rest in God—contemplation. You are no longer doing anything; it is enough simply to be in the Divine Presence.

3. Keep a Journal.

Writing your reflections helps you embody insights and turn them into continuing prayer that can accompany you daily. I use a loose-leaf notebook, but many people prefer one of the beautiful journal books sold in bookstores. Scraps of paper do not work! If you prefer to journal on a computer or electronic tablet, create a journal folder. Some people feel nervous about writing their thoughts, especially if they have had a bad experience with writing in school. Remember that there are no grades for this activity; no one will mark your spelling, syntax, or sentence structure, and unless you choose to share your thoughts no one is going to read your journal. Your journal entries may come directly from reflection on a psalm, but reflection will likely bring other issues to your awareness. I recall a day when, all too soon after chanting the Psalms, a member of the community made a remark I found insensitive and hurtful. Instead of suppressing the anger (my typical way of dealing with it), I began to write in my journal and name what I was feeling. As I did this I realized that the person had not intended to upset me but had opened many old wounds. He had "pushed a button." At the same time he *did* bear some responsibility for what he had said. Feeling much calmer after reflecting in my journal on the situation, I told him how I had experienced his remark. He immediately apologized, and our fellowship was restored. We come to know ourselves better when we take time to journal.

Be Honest

THE PSALMS INVITE US to be honest. Some Christians have difficulty with the imprecatory psalms and would prefer to leave them out of the Bible. Jesus teaches us to love our neighbors and even our enemies, so how can we possibly utter words in which we demand revenge? Rejection of such passages may indicate our unwillingness to deal with feelings of rage and vindictiveness or our prideful desire to be better than the original writers. Of course we don't really intend to murder our enemies—or have God do it for us—but do we not identify with outraged desire for revenge? Speaking such desires to God means leaving them in the hands of our loving Creator, the only one who can be trusted to act with grace toward us and toward those we wish to destroy. Even the imprecatory psalms can have a healing effect on us.

The Psalms come to us from people who desired to walk in God's way and allowed the wisdom of the law to guide their steps. As we read their words and listen to the Voice that inspired them, we discover the blessedness of the journey. And with these ancient psalmists, our minds and hearts are enlightened as we ask God day by day to "Open [our] eyes, so that [we] may behold wondrous things out of your law" (Ps. 119:18).

Give Voice to Daily Experience

THE PSALMISTS WROTE out of their daily experiences. Nothing was too mundane or earth-shattering to bring to God, whether it was caused by pain, ecstatic joy, fear, hope, or longing to know holy

Presence. The author of Psalm 45 celebrates the glory of the royal court and the king as a great warrior anointed by God to rule over a righteous kingdom. The beauty of the princess with her bridesmaids in attendance is described as she comes to the king. The psalm's author can hardly contain his sense of wonder and privilege as he composes verses that are like "the pen of a skilled writer" (v. 1, NIV). When something really grabs us, we may be surprised at our capacity to give voice to the experience. The trouble is that all too often our days pass in busyness without pause to acknowledge the divine grace that touches our lives moment by moment. But if we do stop—even briefly—we notice the gratitude, fear, or other emotion that lies beneath the surface of experience. Out of this awareness we can pray with integrity—and create our own psalms.

It is not as hard as we might imagine to write psalm prayers for our own use or to share in a worship context if we start with the following simple model:

- Take some time to be still, and ask the Spirit of God to show you where you are on the journey of faith. Perhaps today feels like a mountaintop time. Maybe concern for a sick family member or friend is uppermost in your mind. Maybe some situation of injustice disturbs you, loss of a friend or job saddens you, or being let down by a person or organization has angered you. All of these are valid emotional responses and need to be prayed.

- Begin by jotting down any words or phrases that come to mind as you consider the situation. In the case of a sick family member, you might include words and phrases like, *not fair, tears, unresolved issues, gratitude for* (or *dissatisfaction with) a physician, blame, helplessness, waiting, crying out, overwhelming fear,* and *longing for healing.*

- Choose a psalm that relates in some way to your need and allow it to become a template for your prayer. After following a few verses you may find that your psalm takes off on its own, leaving behind the structure of the biblical psalm you started with.

The following example can help you get started. First, read the psalm in its original form; then read the version I wrote based on the psalm's structure:

> You who live in the shelter of the Most High,
>   who abide in the shadow of the Almighty,
> will say to the LORD, "My refuge and my fortress;
>   my God, in whom I trust."
> For he will deliver you from the snare of the fowler
>   and from the deadly pestilence.
> —*Psalm 91:1-3*

∾

> Those who remain at rest in God
> will come to know arms of love encircling them.
> I cry to you, my God, trusting you for help
> and praying for faith in your healing love.
> Please help me to let go of anger
> toward those who have disappointed me.
> Hear my prayer, loving Creator, for one who is sick,
> a suffering one who needs your healing.

The second psalm begins with an image similar to Psalm 91, but takes on its own direction according to the particular need I am bringing before God. Give some thought to the expressions that best name your sense of who God is for you; if *Most High*, *the Almighty*, or *Lord* does not work for you, choose other ways of naming God. In her book *Psalms for Praying: An Invitation to Wholeness*, Nan C. Merrill uses wonderfully creative expressions to address God: Beloved, Living Presence, Gracious One, Bestower of Life, Eternal Listener, Radiant One.[1]

Titles like these may describe how you experience God more realistically than traditional forms of address coined in a different time and cultural context. Feel free to choose a form of address that best fits the desire or prayer you bring before God.

Create New Psalms for Personal Prayer and Worship

THE PSALMS WERE CREATED largely for worship. Our Psalter includes individual cries for help and thanksgiving for deliverance, but even these found a way into the corporate worship of God's people. You may feel intimidated by the suggestion that you create your own psalms, but the model I offer is simple and has been used by youth and seniors alike. At the end of each chapter you are invited to write a psalm of your own, one that includes your experience, desire, need, hope, or joy. You can allow your thoughts to "take off" or use a simple model I learned many years ago.

During the time I served as a parish priest in New York, I accompanied a multigenerational group to Long Island one Saturday. We gathered in a meadow close to the Long Island Sound, and a naturalist led us through the meadow along a path to the shore. Our guide requested that we be silent and walk with awareness. We passed through grasses, wildflowers, bushes, and a few mud puddles. We were instructed to note our observations—the effects of the breeze, the color of the sky, the texture of earth and vegetation, our neighbor's walking—and, when we came to the shore, the little creatures skittering about in the shallow water.

After the walk the group returned to the picnic tables in the meadow where we received a copy of Psalm 104. Our guide asked us to use its structure and write our observations into its pattern. We were not in the mountains of ancient Israel, but we sensed the same holy Presence as the psalmist. We wrote our psalms out of our own experience and gratitude for the order of creation. No wild asses, mountain goats, rock badgers, or whales peopled our psalms, but there were plenty of birds (some of them named), bees, ants, quahogs, and no-see-ums included in our prayer. We celebrated the sun and wind, one another, escape from the city for a few hours, and prayed for a fresh sense of order in our lives when we returned.

There were no grades given for our psalms. Group members ranged in age from three to ninety. All who could write produced something and moved beyond shyness to read their psalm as preparation for a

Eucharist celebrated around a rough-hewn picnic table under the trees. It was one of the highlights of my ministry in New York. This was not about who could produce the best psalm. Instead, it revealed the diversity and inclusiveness of the people of God and moved us to affirm our own experience of the Holy alongside scripture. For some, it opened a new possibility of relating to God in ways that were deeply personal and integrated with daily life and experience.

Back in the city the group members realized how our contemporary psalms could encompass our encounters in corporate life, with dishonest landlords, street people, traffic, and national/political life. Our psalms could help us mourn the death of a friend from AIDS, pray for the bad-tempered bus driver, rage at an unfair job loss, express our fears, and call on God to redress the oppression of those who suffer.

Words are not the only way to express prayer, and sometimes you may want to use color, drawing, or even doodling to pray your experience. This also can be part of your journal, or you may want to have a plain paper pad nearby and some crayons, colored pencils, or oil pastels on hand.

Sometimes it may be appropriate to create new psalms for use in a worship service.

• Identify the theme of the day's scripture readings and spend some time meditating on the biblical stories.

• Note words or images that emerge as you ponder scripture and decide on the main theme(s) and tone of the readings. For example, the familiar story of the prodigal son in Luke 15:11-32 generates words such as *ungrateful, greedy, self-aggrandizement, impatience, compassion, resentment,* and *self-righteousness*. Although we hear more about the younger son and his descent into debauchery and poverty, we also focus on the abundant love and forgiveness of his father and the resentment of the older son. This is a family story we find replicated in many homes today, and it leads us to wonder at the abundant love of the parent, who represents God.

Do we find ourselves in this story? Do any of the characters possess attitudes that we too have adopted?

In his book *The Return of the Prodigal Son: A Story of Homecoming*, Henri J. M. Nouwen spends a significant amount of time identifying with the prodigal and even with the elder brother; it took a member of the community in which he lived to point out that he was called to be the loving father who acted compassionately toward those in the community. Where do you find yourself, your congregation, in this story? Often other scriptures will come to mind, especially verses from the Psalms. David's psalm of penitence fits well with the prodigal's words of penitence:

Have mercy on me, O God,
    according to your steadfast love;
according to your abundant mercy
    blot out my transgressions.
—*Psalm 51:1*

David laments his sinful behavior and asks God for forgiveness. In the story of the prodigal, there is also a returning to God and home after the young man left his family and went into a faraway country. The psalm I offer below picks up the theme of returning to God. Any of us could use it in congregational worship when we become aware of our wandering from the God who loves us:

God of all grace, forgive us when we run from your discipline;
bring us home to ourselves, and give us humility to return.
You have treasured us like a devoted parent, lavishing gifts upon
us; but we have squandered and wasted your blessings.
Holy One, the road home is hard and compels us to let go
of reputation, honor, and a place at your table.
Compassionate God, you meet us with arms outstretched;
you do not punish us for our refusals of your love.
You invite us to feast from your abundance;

you forgive our waywardness and welcome us home.
Deliver us from self-righteousness, O God,
and from harsh judgments on those we despise.
Help us to know that your reconciling grace is for all,
your love beyond our imagining.
Let us bless your holy name forever,
and rejoice to find our place at your table.

With practice you will be able to let go of the biblical psalms as starting points and begin from where you are as the rhythm becomes more familiar. Writing psalms in your journal provides excellent practice, and no one else needs to see them. However, sharing your writing with a trusted friend or family member can be especially encouraging. Finding—or creating—a psalm-sharing group is a blessing.

In a group, begin with a few minutes of quiet reflection and prayer. Then invite one member of the group to read the psalm followed by a brief silence. Then ask people to share, without discussion, a word or phrase that touches them. Another person then reads the same psalm. Then again allow a brief time for reflection on the question, "Where does this speak to me in my life today?" This process works best when we simply listen to one another and save discussion until later. The third reading offers time to think about what God might be asking of us or inviting us into. At this point each can share, followed by discussion together. Individual members of the group might take responsibility for writing a psalm for the group to discuss and amplify, or the psalm writing can be a communal effort from the outset.

Bear in mind that the psalm offered for use in a worship service will address contemporary forms of old stories, so the discussion should identify current issues.

TWO

Hearing God's Word
in Stillness and Silence

"Be still, and know that I am God!"
Psalm 46:10

FOR FOUR YEARS I lived in Manhattan, "the city that never sleeps." Early each morning garbage trucks banged trash cans beneath my window, taxis blared their horns, and metal store shutters screeched open. Throughout the day people rushed about their business—myself included—on and off the subway, riding the buses, hailing and sometimes fighting to get a cab. I heard greetings and curses, emergency vehicle sirens, the hot dog vendor shouting enticements, the mentally challenged homeless people trying to snag passersby. And this was before the advent of the cell phone! I loved the vibrancy and energy of the city but sometimes longed for a place of stillness. That longing has increased over the years. I yearn to be still and aware of holy Presence. Living now in the mountains of North Carolina, I experience far less noise and have a more relaxed pace of life, but the stillness I long for often eludes me. Outwardly it may be quiet, but my busy mind and body hold me back from stillness.

"Be still, and know that I am God!" The author of Psalm 46 hears the voice of the Creator calling out in the midst of life's struggles. The psalm begins with a reminder that God is a refuge and strength in times of cataclysmic storm surges that bring terror to the people of

God. For most Middle Eastern people, the sea served as a powerful image of disorder, death, and the fear of being overwhelmed by chaos. Though the people of Israel lived along the fertile Mediterranean coast, they never succeeded in becoming a seafaring nation. When King Solomon needed timber to build his lavish palace and the Temple, he negotiated with the King of Tyre to ship cedars to Israel since Israel owned no vessels in which to transport goods. The Israelites would not understand our glossy calendar pictures of calm oceans inviting us to meditation and stillness. They would more likely see the ocean as oppressive—"All your waves and your billows have gone over me" (Ps. 42:7). People regarded the sea as a dangerous place, even in Jesus' time. When the author of Revelation wanted to express the tranquility of a new heaven and earth, he wrote, "Then I saw a new heaven and a new earth; for the first heaven and the first earth had passed away, and *the sea was no more*" (Rev. 21:1, emphasis added).

Psalm 46 provides reassurance that, despite earth-shattering events and warfare, God is Defender of the people. Reciting this hope together strengthens trust and leads to the confident note on which the psalm ends: "The LORD of hosts is with us; the God of Jacob is our refuge" (v. 11). Tucked into this song of turmoil comes this invitation: "'Be still, and know that I am God. I am exalted among the nations, I am exalted in the earth!'" (v. 10). In times of destruction and powerlessness, God's people remember that they do not have the whole picture. Despite encroaching fear they are able to be still, to know that God is God, and to remember in whose world they live. Instead of striving to change the way things are, they ponder God's presence and power in the cosmos.

To be still in the midst of conflict is a challenge. Back in the early eighties, I returned to my native England as a newly ordained priest. The Church of England did not ordain women and I found myself frenetically busy talking to the media and meeting with various groups. Sometimes I celebrated the Eucharist in private homes. One of those homes was the deanery of Saint Paul's Cathedral, where a group of clergy gathered early one morning, some of them with questions on their minds about the ordination of women. By that time my ego was well and truly in control. No one was denied an interview. The press, TV, radio, and the Movement for the Ordination of Women all wanted a piece of me, and, like a crusader, I gladly responded.

When the Eucharist ended that morning, an older priest asked if I had time to accompany him to his church in the City of London. We stepped out into the foggy morning and walked the few blocks to the ancient building where he led me down a narrow flight of stairs into the crypt. It was a small space sparsely furnished with about a dozen chairs. He sat down on the front row and invited me to join him. I had no idea what he might have to say. Did he need to talk about his own difficulty with women's ordination? Had he suffered some personal trial he needed to talk about? Might he want to make a confession? For a long time I waited for him to speak, but he said nothing. We both faced the altar with a cross on the stone wall behind it. That seemed to be the focus of his attention. I followed his gaze, uncomfortable with the silence, longing for him to tell me why we were there. And still the silence continued. Finally I began to notice a change in my body and from deep within tears welled up as I realized that this priest was not asking me for anything; he was giving me a precious gift, the gift of stillness and silence. As we sat quietly in that place of prayer I was able to pause long enough to recognize my arrogance, self-indulgence, and the busyness that I thought was ministry. "Be still, and know that I am God!" was exactly the unspoken message I needed to set me back on track with the awareness that my call was to God's service and not to self-aggrandizement.

Another psalm reference to stillness in God's presence appears in Psalm 131:3: "I still my soul and make it quiet, like a child upon its mother's breast; my soul is quieted within me." The suckling child is helpless, dependent on its mother, and, in this image, rests content in its mother's arms. Even as toddlers we continue to rest in the arms of our mothers (and fathers) because there we find safety, love, and nurture. Who has not been held tenderly upon waking from a scary dream or loved the intimacy of enfolding arms during bedtime stories? The psalm suggests that, as God's little ones, we are invited to rest trustingly in the divine arms, aware of our need for protection and nurture as we choose to become still. But how do we become still? Often I carry busyness rather than stillness into prayer. I must remember the people and places I have promised to pray for and get on with the business of asking God to fix their various needs. I become so busy talking to God that I forget to listen to what God may be saying to me: "Be still, and know that I am God; lean on me, rest in me, receive strength and grace. Take time to still your soul, to become quiet so that I can sing you a lullaby." And for a moment I stop the spoken prayers and enter into a deeper kind of praying in which I listen to the Holy One instead of babbling requests. I have to keep returning to the stillness because all too soon my busy mind takes over again.

The writer of Psalm 16 expresses deep trust in God who protects, guides, satisfies, and enfolds him. He goes on to say, "Therefore my heart is glad, and my soul rejoices; my body also rests secure" (Ps. 16:9). Heart, soul, and body are profoundly interwoven as the psalmist rests in God in whose presence there is "fullness of joy" (Ps. 16:11). This kind of stillness is countercultural. We in the Western hemisphere pride ourselves on being busy, staying active, and spending ourselves at work. The weekend finds us busy in the yard, cleaning house, shopping, and perhaps filling some of the "spare" time with entertainment. Often we end up so exhausted by the busyness that we opt for some kind of mind-numbing activity—alcohol, drugs, television—and stillness is the last thing on our minds. This lifestyle is ultimately debilitating and leads to all sorts of maladies—physical, psychological, and spiritual. For twenty-first-century Western people, questions arise when we consider taking time out for stillness: "Since this is the culture in which I live, how can I realistically find time for stillness?" "What will happen if I stop what I am doing and become still?" "Will I hear God speak in the stillness?" "I was punished by silence as a child; how can I overcome my fear of being still?" These legitimate questions deserve our attention as we seek to move more deeply into God's love.

We may have to overcome resistance to becoming still and quiet in God's presence. Many of us carry unconscious images of God as a distant deity or a rigid schoolmaster waiting to catch us out and punish us for our failures. We may have heard sermons that focus on sin and our separation from the God of wrath. I grew up in a church where we were encouraged to address God as Father but also taught that original sin would always manifest itself in our imperfect lives; therefore, we could never be good enough. It took me many years to shift my awareness to the more nurturing, enfolding Mother-God image of Psalm 131. No one image of God can begin to express the awesome mystery of our Creator, but bringing to consciousness the images that have controlled our thought and influenced our prayer can open a doorway into a deeper relationship with God. This shift may take time and require practice as little by little we allow time for quiet, listening prayer.

A key word here is *listening*. We tend to think of prayer as talking to God, whether in adoration or intercession, thanksgiving or confession. But what if God wants to begin the conversation? Reading the Psalms or any other part of scripture with a listening heart is transformative and takes us deeper into the heart of God. If this kind of prayer is challenging, begin with a short time, preferably before the busy day begins. Then gradually increase the length of time in prayer. Let go of expectations. Sometimes the time will pass quickly and you will be focused, but more likely busy thoughts will interrupt you often and rarely will you receive blinding visions. Instead, the intentionality of regular practice will begin to draw you into a place where you are enfolded by grace.

Praying with Our Bodies

WHEN HE WRITES to Christians in Rome, Paul appeals to them: "present your bodies as a living sacrifice, holy and acceptable to God, which is your spiritual worship" (Rom. 12:1). Paying attention to our bodies is prayer, not just a prelude to traditional prayer; it is spiritual worship. In our Western tradition we have tended to separate body and mind, even to despise the body. But in earlier times, not only the Hebrews, but Christians too celebrated God's image in our bodies. One of the most radical expressions of the profound connection between our bodies and the Christ presence is found in a hymn by Saint Symeon the New Theologian, a mystic and monastic priest who lived from 949–1022.

> We become members of Christ—and Christ becomes our members,
> Christ becomes my hand, Christ, my miserable foot....
> I move my hand, and my hand is the whole Christ
> since, do not forget it, God is indivisible in His divinity.[1]

In light of this poem, who would not wish to celebrate the awesomeness of the body and to pray bodily through and with the Word who became flesh and lived among us (John 1:14)? Who would not long to be soul-quiet and rest on God's nurturing breast?

In order to move the focus of our prayers from asking to listening, we need practices that enable us to still body as well as mind. If our bodies are tense or if we are agitated, it is likely that our minds will be unfocused. The Hebrew people prayed with their bodies, and many of the psalms were written for processions, dance, and ritual drama. We too can embrace body prayer and discover how it leads us into stillness of mind. Some of our churches may offer liturgical dance, but for many of us there is little corporate embodiment of worship. Perhaps this is why Palm Sunday processions are so popular. We can, however, incorporate our bodies into our own times of prayer. The following exercise can become a helpful, regular prelude to listening prayer.

Begin with a few stretches reaching up, opening the arms, and then placing your open hands together in a posture of receiving. Repeat the stretches several times and pay attention to your breath. Allow your breathing to become deeper and slower. When you are ready, sit in a comfortable chair that offers good back support, place your feet on the floor with your hands open in your lap. Continue to observe your breathing, and become aware of how your body feels.

Begin relaxing by focusing on your feet and gradually moving up your legs, torso, neck, and head, consciously relaxing each area. Sometimes you will notice that tension or pain exists even after relaxation; in your mind go back to that place, tighten the muscles around the pain center, and then let go. By this time your regular breathing rhythm will help you to be still, and you can begin to repeat the phrase: "Be still, and know that I am God." It is helpful to speak aloud if it does not disturb anyone else. Another way to use this mantra[2] is to leave off a word each time it is repeated so that it looks like this:

Be still and know that I am God
Be still and know that I am
Be still and know
Be still
Be

Praying with Others

ONE SUNDAY EVENING A month my church offers a service of quiet reflection in the tradition of Taizé.[3] I love this time of worship because it offers brief periods of silence that follow the singing of a chant, usually based on words of scripture. I also love it because I am not alone in the silence. I have been in many prayer groups, but sometimes these have been noisy affairs with barely a pause for breath between each petition. It also seemed that the prayers offered were more informational for those of us in the group than the holding of a person or situation in the Light of God. It is a deep and wonderful experience to wait in the wordless stillness with others, knowing that God needs not my input but my presence in order to bless others and take care of the world.

Creating a group willing to meet for silent waiting before God is not difficult for most of us. Two or three like-minded people and a regular time to gather are enough, at least to begin with. It helps to check in briefly with one another (which is not the same as chitchat) and then begin the time of silence by lighting a candle, listening to gentle music, or saying/singing a chant together. Have one person serve as timekeeper to free others from wondering when the time is up. A chime or bell is a great tool for indicating it is time to finish.

SUGGESTIONS FOR REFLECTION ∾

Decide on a time each day you can "interrupt" your busyness by spending five minutes with a mantra—either "Be still, and know that I am God" or one you create for yourself.

PSALM PRAYER
    God of wind and tempest,
    God of the still small voice,
    Help me to quiet my mind
    and let go of busy thoughts.
    I yearn for stillness in your presence;
    I want to sit at your feet like Mary
    and listen deeply to your wisdom.
    Help me to let go without worry.
    Let my heart be ready to host you.
    Gracious God, I come to you as I am,
    ready to become your listening child.

WRITING A PSALM ∾

As you have read this chapter, what experiences of quiet resting have come to mind? Perhaps you recall a childhood moment when you were safely held in love or a place that is special to you because it represents peaceful resting. How do you feel about such experiences? Be still for a few minutes, and let these memories surface; then write a sentence or two to express your appreciation. From what you have written, begin to create your own psalm. Remember that if finding a structure is difficult to begin with, you can take one of the Hebrew psalms and change the images to reflect your experience.

THREE

Resting
in God's Grace

Return, O my soul, to your rest.
Psalm 116:7

T HE DISCIPLES OF JESUS return from a successful mission and
tell him all that they have done and taught (Mark 6:30). They
have gone out with only a staff—no money, no food, no bag to carry
goods, trusting that God would supply their needs. Previously they
had watched Jesus respond to the sick, listened to his parables; and
when he called them to carry the good news into other towns and
villages, they readily said yes. It must have been a heady time as they
experienced the people gladly listening to what they had to say and
saw the sick healed and the poor given hope. Now they are full of
stories to tell Jesus and probably a bit full of themselves, expecting his
words of approval. Instead he says to them, "Come away to a deserted
place all by yourselves and rest a while" (Mark 6:31). The disciples
need a time of renewal, a place to rest and reflect on who they are
and whom they serve.

Jesus recognizes that his followers cannot sustain the mission
on adrenalin alone, and he shows them a vital rhythm for the life of
faith and service. It is a rhythm they have seen him practice. When
the crowds came to him day after day, even late into the evening,
Mark tells us, "In the morning, while it was still very dark, he got up

and went out to a deserted place, and there he prayed" (Mark 1:35). Jesus sets an important example for us in this passage and in others where he dismisses the crowd and withdraws to a place where he can rest. Matthew 14:23 does not suggest that Jesus waits until everyone has had all their needs taken care of before he withdraws, and Luke 5:15-16 states that he heads for the wilderness even while great crowds surround him.

In an age noted for its speed, with countless gadgets to enable us to achieve instant results, many of us keep going like the busy squirrels in our yards. I have noticed with shame that when someone asks me, "How are you?" I all too often respond by telling them how busy I am. Unconsciously I want to convey my success, to let the inquirer know that I am very busy about God's work. Only when I take time to go to my own desert place do I see the response for what it is. My motivation becomes conscious, and I must bring it to God for forgiveness. I offer a prayer for help to remember that it is only by the grace of God that I can faithfully respond to the call to serve. One of the reasons I stay so busy is that "no" rarely enters my vocabulary. I try to be "omnicompetent." Or to put it more harshly, I try to be God.

Rest for the Soul

THE SCRIPTURES ARE FULL of invitations to rest. Psalm 116 celebrates the writer's recovery from illness. He expresses his love for the God who has listened to his pleas for healing. God has been gracious and merciful, protecting him and lifting him up from a near-death experience. Now he admonishes himself: "Return, O my soul, to your rest, for the LORD has dealt bountifully with you" (Ps. 116:7). God's grace is bountiful; the more we take time to reflect on our lives, the more we see each day's gifts in the midst of our busyness. Times of distress or sickness but also small events—the handwritten message sent through the mail, a shared meal, a smile from the checkout clerk, new growth in the garden—speak of God's bounty. There is more than a little wisdom in the old song, "Count your blessings, name them one by one, and it will surprise you what the Lord hath done."[1]

Restlessness seems to characterize our way of life in the West. We scurry from one church meeting to another, keep ourselves busy with serving the poor, young people, shut-ins, and the church office, but sometimes we forget to rest in God. Brief reading of a daily devotion booklet and prayer begin our day, and then we are up and running to get everything done. And maybe there is some of the self-congratulation the disciples felt hidden like a "snake in the grass" waiting to encourage our inflated egos. "Return, O my soul, to your rest" is an imperative that nudges us not only after a time of suffering but also in the midst of our good work for God.

During visits to Southern Africa, I have noticed how relaxed the people in rural areas seem to be. Many of them live in townships where poorly constructed shacks provide the only housing, and there are few of the facilities that we take for granted. Women at the common tap gather with their buckets, and in the evening families sit around a campfire and tell stories. I am not suggesting that the poverty they suffer is to be preferred to our taken-for-granted wealth, but it does appear that greater contentment and community life is a norm.

We can support one another on the soul-journey and offer encouragement in times of pain or restlessness. A *lectio divina* group began in my church a couple of years ago, and all those who joined are faithful members of the community, each with a specific ministry. They are busy people who have discovered that their souls are thirsty for a deeper relationship with God, and so they committed to ninety minutes each week to reflect together on scripture and to enter into Centering Prayer. The time spent together has become a transformative experience that has led to a desire for more teaching and a longer, restful time of retreat. Now the group also gathers once a quarter in a member's home where we practice Centering Prayer, *lectio divina*, and a time of silence for reflection. We have discovered together that we need this balance of work and prayer in order to stay faithful as we care for our own soul-life. David wrote of God as the Shepherd who led him to places of refreshment—green pastures and still waters—where "he restores my soul" (Ps. 23:3). Soul restoration is a necessity for each of us as a counterbalance to busyness that can drain us of the life-giving wisdom of God.

Sometimes the rest we long for does not come as quickly as desired. In Psalm 130 the writer finds himself in "the depths" of disappointment as he waits for God to act. "I wait for the LORD, my soul waits and in his word I hope; my soul waits for the Lord" (Ps. 130:5-6). While he waits with his restless soul, the psalmist maintains hope because he trusts in the promises recorded in the word of God. One of the verses of scripture I memorized in Sunday school was Proverbs 3:5-6. "Trust in the LORD with all your heart, and do not rely on your own insight. In all your ways acknowledge him, and he will make straight your paths." I hoped in that text many times when I was "in the depths" or just plain exhausted and restless, and I am glad that we were encouraged to memorize scripture. The word of God, treasured in the heart, is accessible to us at all times. Our hope lies in the trust that, while difficulties encompass us, God is gracious, and we remain hope-filled even as we yearn for rest.

It has been suggested that a good rule of thumb for our times with God is "an hour a day, a day a month, and a week a year." Each of us must decide an appropriate rhythm of prayer and rest according to our circumstances. I have found that taking time out for retreat is invaluable, whether for a weekend or a full week, though there is no guarantee of immediate deliverance from fatigue and restlessness! The first twenty-four hours of a retreat are often a time of unwinding, letting go, and recognizing our fatigue. If the retreat is in a religious house, it can be a blessing to be present at the times of worship, which often include chanting, that can form a background for personal prayer. In fact, it may be the only prayer we have. Instead of trying to maintain our usual pattern of prayer, we may simply allow the community to pray for and through us. Often our body is tired and needs rest too. Sitting on the porch in a rocker, taking short walks, stretching, or even sleeping moves us into a more receptive posture before God.

Psalm 16 is a song of trust and security in God. The writer asks for protection, delights himself in holy people, and is clear that he has chosen God over all the idols in the land. "Therefore my heart is glad, and my soul rejoices; my body also rests secure" (Ps. 16:9). We have already considered Paul's words to Christians in Rome to present their bodies as a living sacrifice to God because this is *spiritual worship* (Rom. 12:1). The troubled Corinthian church also received instruction about how to view their bodies: "Your body is a temple of the Holy Spirit within you, which you have from God.... therefore glorify God in your body" (1 Cor. 6:19-20). Francis of Assisi called his body "Brother Ass." He was very harsh in his discipline: sleeping without pallet and fasting beyond reasonableness. At the end of his life, he realized that this was not a gospel way to live and repented of the ill done to his body by abuse. We need to cherish our bodies as God's gift and remember that the Incarnation makes abundantly clear that God honors our humanity.

Many retreat centers today offer massage therapy alongside spiritual guidance and creative activities. These houses of prayer lead us toward a greater wholeness of body, mind, and spirit and show us that if we neglect our physical and psychological well-being, our spirituality withers. We need to recover the reverence and joy of the sabbath that the Hebrew people celebrated. Like every other spiritual practice, such as church attendance on Sunday, sabbath can become a ritual to be accomplished rather than a restful time with God; but it represents an essential need in our lives. When do we take rest on a regular basis? Where do time out and worshipful presence with God figure in our homes? In his book *Sabbath: Finding Rest, Renewal, and Delight in Our Busy Lives*, Wayne Muller tells the story of a young couple starting out in their first home and the generous gift of a washing machine given by the bride's grandparents. They were told it was a Jewish washer. When they asked what that meant, the grandfather explained that it wouldn't work on Shabbat![2] Perhaps it is time for us to consider how in the Christian church our lives may more fully reflect God's creation of a day of rest each week. Maybe there are devices we could do without in order to be more available to God, sacred meals we could institute in our homes, special people we could honor at our table on the sabbath.

Holy Restlessness

BEFORE WE LEAVE THE TOPIC of finding rest for our souls, we need also to consider what seems to be a contradiction. Those who find rest in God discover a restlessness that draws them ever deeper into the divine reality. Knowing God creates a longing, a holy longing, to enter more deeply into relationship with our Creator. Yearning for God is expressed vividly in Psalm 42:

> As a deer longs for flowing streams,
> so my soul longs for you, O God.
> My soul thirsts for God,
> for the living God (vv. 1-2).

The psalmist does not cry out to an unknown deity to help him but to the God of the Hebrew people, the living God who shepherds and sustains him. The Torah is studied as the source of Israel's relationship with God, and those who walk in God's law delight in it because it reveals the good way that is filled with Yahweh's blessing. The longest song in our Psalter, 119, pours out delight in God's law and expresses a restless longing to embody it more and more. "My soul is consumed with longing for your ordinances at all times.... I find my delight in your commandments.... How sweet are your words to my taste, sweeter than honey to my mouth" (vv. 20, 47, 103). The word of God spoke hope and belonging to God's ancient people and inspired their trust even in times of struggle.

Augustine of Hippo famously said that God made us for Godself, and our hearts are restless till they find their rest in God. Those of us who embrace the Christian tradition find that rest not only in the written word but in Jesus the Word made flesh who offers this invitation:

> Come to me, all you that are weary and are carrying heavy burdens, and I will give you rest. Take my yoke upon you, and learn from me; for I am gentle and humble in heart, and you will

find rest for your souls. For my yoke is easy, and my burden is light (Matt. 11:28-30).

Jesus appears to be familiar with the words of Wisdom recorded in Sirach 6:24-31, where the writer calls upon those who would know and serve God to be yoked with Wisdom (God's feminine form). "Come to her with all your soul, and keep her ways.... for at last you will find the rest she gives, and she will be changed into joy for you. Then her fetters will become for you a strong defense" (vv. 26, 28-29). Resting in God becomes possible when we accept the yoke of discipline, the discipline of taking time apart, building into our busy lives desert places of refreshment.

Reflection on Psalm 37 can lead to an awareness that we choose the way we will live in response to events that cause distress. Many of the psalms offer two ways of life, but only one leads to rest and the way of patient trust. "Take delight in the LORD, and he will give you the desires of your heart. Commit your way to the LORD; trust in him and he will act.... Be still before the LORD, and wait patiently for him" (vv. 4-5, 7). The King James Version of the Bible renders verse 7 in words made familiar by Felix Mendelssohn's *Elijah:* "Rest in the LORD, and wait patiently for him." The psalmist's words ring true today and in every age. When the events of our lives move us into excitement, disappointment, anxiety, expectancy, or fear, it is time to return to our rest in God, knowing that all things are held in the arms of the Shepherd of our souls.

SUGGESTIONS FOR REFLECTION ∿

Take several days to meditate on Psalm 37, allowing yourself to hear the words of the writer in your context. Who do you identify as "the wicked"? What causes you to be fretful? How might you be intentional in taking times for rest and returning to life lived in the abundance of God's grace?

Remind me to rest, gracious God,
for I am too busy about your work.
I long for seasons of refreshing
but keep going beyond my strength.
Draw me into your holy presence
where I can stop and be like a child
at peace on its parent's lap
content and safe from all cares.

WRITING A PSALM 〜

Where do you notice restlessness in yourself? What do you long to receive from God in order to return to your soul-rest? Begin to name the restless feelings and to remember times of past returning to repose in God. What do you need from God in order to enter again into a restful place? Begin your psalm by naming those needs. It may be that you feel at rest right now. If so, create a psalm of thanksgiving for the grace that keeps you there.

FOUR

Finding Stability
in God's Faithfulness

The LORD is my rock.
Psalm 18:2

O N A WET AND WINDY DAY in North Wales, a group of friends gathered at the base of an almost sheer rock face. Wet and windy is typical weather in this part of the British Isles, so hikers and climbers shrug, dress appropriately, and go on with their planned activity. I still own the orange oiled Norwegian fisherman's jacket that kept me dry through many journeys in the mountains.

On this particular day our group was learning the techniques of rock climbing, moving on from lectures to the actual experience of making our way up the rock face. When my turn came I was excited, anticipating a flawless climb to the top. I got into my harness and began the climb, remembering instructions about always keeping three points of contact with the rock and engaging my boot in crevasses, some almost invisible. I did very well until about halfway to the top when the rain was pouring down the rock and down my neck. A small misstep and I lost contact with the rock and found myself dangling at the end of the rope being blown from side to side by the wind. It was humiliating and terrifying. My fellow climbers stood below offering advice and encouragement, most of which I could not hear. I shouted to the lead climber at the top, asking him to let me down a couple of feet so I could stand on a ledge to rethink the rest of the ascent. Unfortunately he could not hear me! I remained in that pendulous state for several minutes, though it seemed like hours. Eventually I regained my footing and made it to the top without further mishap. The relief I felt as the lead climber greeted me and the waiting climbers below applauded was glorious. Somehow I forgot the feelings of fear and vulnerability that had gripped me on the upward climb. I stood on solid rock, safe and unconcerned about the wind and rain that continued throughout the day.

At a conference in Atlanta, I heard Anne Lamott suggest that there are two prayers essential to the Christian way, and both are short: "Help!" and "Thank you." On the evening she addressed us, she said that "Help!" had been her frequent prayer as she traveled to Atlanta suffering from a feverish cold and sore throat. I recalled swinging across the wet rock face and realized I had prayed both prayers that day. I cried to God for help and a number of verses from the Psalms flashed through my mind: "Lead me to the rock that is higher than I" (Ps. 61:2). Please God, get me to the top! "[God] set my feet upon a rock, making my steps secure" (Ps. 40:2). You did it for the ancient psalmist, now help me to stop slipping and sliding about and give my feet some traction. Help! Help! Help! Then at the top, with the struggle behind me, Thank you! Thank you! Thank you!

The great rock outcrop where we were climbing was majestic, and from its summit the sea was visible—on a clear day! It was part of the Snowdonia range—rugged, challenging, and very beautiful. Wildflowers bloomed abundantly, and sheep roamed the hills or gathered round to peer at us when we stopped to picnic in one of the meadows or beside a creek. It was easy to sense holy Presence on one of the rare rainless days, but on the day of our climb I understood what the psalmists meant when they wrote of God as a Rock. The rock simply was. Invincible, steadfast, and invitational, it rose up from the earth in ancient magnificence. *Like God*, I thought, *unchanging through the weather of my experiences.*

When I feel unstable because a colleague who likes to argue and point out my Christian naiveté challenges my faith, God is my Rock. When a big storm arises at home and my father accuses me of religious mania because I go to church more than once a week, God is my Rock. And when I slip, and my failure is visible to all, God is my Rock.

We may find ourselves unstable and feeling disconnected from the Rock of our salvation (Ps. 62:2), swinging across the face of the Rock but with no solid contact. There are seasons of life when turbulence is such that we lose our footing and forget that the Rock has not changed. I found myself in a place like this when, at very short notice, the priory where I had lived and served for over five years was slated to be closed. During the time I lived there, I had grown accustomed to and appreciative of the divine office—the gathering of the community five times each day for prayer and worship. Sometimes I may not have felt like going to church to sing the psalms and listen to scripture once again, but I found a great blessing in the routine. It provided a solid foundation to our life together, and often the wisdom of the appointed psalm seemed to speak to me in a direct way. I was going to lose all of this. The ground beneath me felt wobbly. To begin with, I had no idea of the direction my life would take and no clear sense of God's call to new ministry. One thing had not changed: God remained faithful and trustworthy, and I needed to keep reminding myself of this truth even when I did not feel it.

Since my early teens I have read and reflected on scripture daily, and I celebrate the blessing of coming to know and trust God's word. When life is challenging, I remember that so many of the people we read of in scripture went through uncertain and difficult times, and their stories reveal the grace and faithfulness of God. When faith is shaky, we remember all that God has done in the past for others and also for us, and we build on the foundation of God our Rock so that the house of our faith will stand no matter what storms beat against it (Matt. 7:24-27).

Psalm 19 celebrates the awesome power of God in a creation that speaks silently of the greatness of the Creator.

The heavens are telling the glory of God;
  and the firmament proclaims [God's] handiwork.
Day to day pours forth speech,
  and night to night declares knowledge.
There is no speech, nor are there words;
  their voice is not heard;
yet their voice goes out through all the earth,
  and their words to the end of the world.
—*Psalm 19:1-4*

We have only to ponder the wonders of creation to see and hear God's good word addressed to us through the beauty, the wildness, and the imagination that breathed the world into being. Creation is like God's first book, but then we also have the law of God to guide us and bring us to fullness of life. The author of the psalm goes on to say that the law (word) of God is perfect, sure, right, clear, pure, true; and studying it brings wisdom, rejoicing, and enlightenment. These words of God are "more to be desired…than gold, even much fine gold; sweeter also than honey, and drippings of the honeycomb" (v. 10). The writer says that creation and the written word of God speak clearly of who God is and what God asks of us. The rabbis insist that study of the law is fundamental to Judaism; repetition embeds the word of God within the heart and mind. Likewise our study of the word in creation and scripture shapes us in Christian faith and sustains us in adversity. The psalm ends with a well-known prayer: "Let the words of my mouth and the meditation of my heart be acceptable to you, O LORD, my rock and my redeemer" (v. 14). Perhaps we associate this prayer with the words spoken by a minister before the sermon, but what might happen if we prayed it daily? Perhaps we would be challenged to speak gospel truth, to focus our thoughts on what is "good and acceptable and perfect" (Rom. 12:2). Perhaps we would allow ourselves to be transformed by the word dwelling in us.

Rock of Ages

THE HEBREW SCRIPTURES OFTEN portrayed God as a Rock, as one who is steadfast, trustworthy, and sheltering. "Ascribe greatness to our God! The Rock, [God's] work is perfect," proclaims Moses in Deuteronomy 32:3-4; and the Psalms contain numerous references to God as the Rock of the people.

> Hear my cry, O God;
>> listen to my prayer.
> From the end of the earth I call to you,
>> when my heart is faint.
> Lead me to the rock that is higher than I;
>> for you are my refuge.
> —*Psalm 61:1-3*

It is in times of difficulty, surrounded by enemies or storms, that we are drawn to the certainty that God is stronger than we are, rocklike and dependable. God provides many safe places in the turbulent experiences of our lives and holds us safe until the storm is over.

Psalm 18 is distinguished from other songs because it appears twice in the Hebrew scriptures. The first version is in 2 Samuel 22:2-51 where it is identified as David's song of thanksgiving and occurs after he is delivered from Saul. David's followers declare that David should no longer go in harm's way. The version in Psalm 18 appears to be for the whole community, whereas in Second Samuel it is David who personally claims God's rocklike presence in his life. Jewish tradition associates the psalm with the seventh day of Passover, when God split the sea, the climax of redemption from Egypt, and pointed toward the ultimate redemption by God. God the Rock, who brought the people out of slavery, sustained them in the wilderness, and raised up leaders to gather them into a community of faith, would ultimately triumph over the forces of evil and bring victory beyond any earthly success.

Hymn writers have frequently used the metaphor of God, or Christ, as the Rock foundation of Christian people. The eighteenth-century Anglican cleric Augustus M. Toplady wrote many hymns, and tradition has it that his most famous hymn, "Rock of Ages," was composed after he experienced a severe storm when he was out walking in the Somerset countryside. Looking around for a place of refuge, Toplady noticed a crevice in a rock that appeared to be split in two and climbed up into its narrow shelter. There he waited out the storm and later pondered the experience, using the imagery of the rock to speak of Christ's work of salvation.

The split rock in which the Calvinist preacher Toplady sheltered caused him to think about the suffering, pierced side, and death of Christ as the means of our salvation. I remember climbing up into the crevice that local lore claimed was the very site of Toplady's shelter and later lustily singing his hymn, "Rock of Ages, cleft for me." It became a favorite of mine, especially during the turmoil of adolescence and "stormy weather" at home. I could look to Christ as the person and place of stability.

Edward Mote, a nineteenth-century hymn writer who became a Baptist minister, wrote the hymn "My Hope Is Built," with the familiar chorus:

On Christ, the solid Rock, I stand:
all other ground is sinking sand.

Mote, who like me grew up in an English pub, was left as a child to rely on himself and found his own way into the life of faith. I identify with his journey. My mother did her best to raise us, but my father was rarely available since he was responsible for the pub 365 days a year and never took a vacation. I give thanks to God that I met some people of faith while I was in high school and found my way into the church community.

God is our Rock. In God's faithfulness we have stability. Sometimes I may find myself dangling at the edge of the Rock wondering if I will ever get my feet back on the firm ground that is God. Sometimes I may have to endure a struggle because I have taken a misstep that has landed me in a slippery place. But God's promises are enduring:

[God] drew me up from the desolate pit,
  out of the miry bog,
and set my feet upon a rock,
  making my steps secure.
—*Psalm 40:2*

SUGGESTIONS FOR REFLECTION ⤮

Read the rest of Psalm 40 as a meditation. Where do you see yourself in the psalmist's experience? Notice the writer's response in this psalm to the redeeming work of God.

PSALM PRAYER

  Steady me, God, help me to stay firm
  on the Rock that is Christ.
  Lift me up when I fall;
  strengthen me when I fear.
  Please remind me always
  that you are stronger than all my enemies.

WRITING A PSALM ⤮

Consider times when you have felt unstable on your faith journey and have discovered that Christ is the Rock beneath you. Did you cry out for help? Were there others who helped you rediscover the firm foundation on which faith is based? How did you learn that God remained faithful? You might begin the psalm with a statement such as this: O God, your faithfulness is beyond measure...

FIVE

Dealing with Disappointment, Anger, and Pain

How long, O Lord?
Psalm 13:1

H ow long will it take us to get there?" asked my six-year-old nephew as we drove to a restaurant for supper one evening. "About two Tom and Jerrys," replied his father, who knew that thirty minutes was an impossible concept for Christopher but would make sense measured in the length of a TV cartoon. Later, as I thought about the question, I realized it often applied to me on my faith journey. How long will it take me to overcome this fear, to know the next step on my journey, to see healing for a friend, to deal with a broken relationship? In my prayers I ask, "How long, O Lord?" but God does not tell me how many Tom and Jerrys it will take. Often the question seems to be met with silence and an invitation to wait. In the meantime, I may wonder if God is really aware of my need for help or whether I am forgotten; after all, my requests must seem so small to the Creator of the universe. Perhaps I did not pray clearly enough or earnestly enough, and maybe I need to remind God that I am here and that I am waiting.

The psalmist was certainly in such a place when he composed Psalm 13, and he was more than a little disappointed in Yahweh.

> How long, O LORD? Will you forget me forever?
> How long will you hide your face from me?
> —*Psalm 13:1*

Psalm 13 is attributed to David but had and has relevance far beyond his time. It speaks to the experience of exile, which the people of God suffered on more than one occasion, and became a cry from the community. The exhausted nation lost energy, felt despair, and cried out to God, "How long?" The dominant power brokers had displaced the people of Israel, who saw no end to the oppression. David's Jerusalem was lost to them and the Temple, which represented the center of their worship, was no longer accessible. How long would they be deserted and forgotten? Later, early Christians would likely find this psalm relevant to their suffering persecution in the Roman world as they continued to recite the Psalter in their gatherings for worship and waited for the fulfillment of Jesus' words about his return.

Today we too sometimes feel forgotten by the God who is at the heart of our faith, but convention has taught us to suppress such experiences. All too often we sanitize Christian prayer to exclude the expressions of anger, disappointment, doubt, and resentment we feel when God seems not to answer our cries for help. Perhaps we forget the words of Jesus from the cross: "My God, my God, why have you forsaken me?" (Ps. 22:1). His cry of anguish was real; his questioning of God was flung out into the universe as he endured excruciating pain and gradual suffocation. If we need permission to join our Jewish brothers and sisters in questioning God, it is surely given in this agonized cry of Jesus.

As a pastor I am often at the bedside of devoted Christians who are suffering horribly. They are people of faith who have greeted me at the door each Sunday with a smile and reassurance that all is well. Many of them have prayed publicly offering thanksgiving and trust to God; but now, in a situation of great suffering, they are puzzled and disappointed. Where is God? Why do I no longer feel loved and strong in faith? And with the questions comes guilt. I am a bad Christian because I question God's love and feel resentful that God does not seem to meet me in this place of suffering. I should stand firm in faith and certainly not verbalize my anger toward God or suggest that I am forgotten. In light of such pain, we must resist the temptation to utter platitudes like Job's "friends" or to make promises that things will change. Instead, we pray silently within and refuse to run from the discomfort of waiting with the suffering one. To wait alongside our sister or brother is to make visible the Christ-presence. We offer the embrace of love and affirm the prayer of the sufferer, who may well be feeling guilty for doubting God's compassion.

Waiting for God

WAITING IS ONE OF the most difficult and most godlike parts of our experience. It is often hard because it reminds us that we have not arrived, that we are unfinished, and that the present moment encompasses the "not yet" of faith. And waiting is frequently made more challenging by the fear of what may be or doubt that waiting will be rewarded by joy. Is it possible that God is waiting for the *kairos*, the right moment, in us? The scriptures bear witness to the God who waits again and again for the right moment to act in the life of the community or an individual. That waiting is especially poignant as God takes flesh in the body of a young woman and becomes subject to the nine months of pregnancy. "When the fullness of time had come, God sent his Son, born of a woman, born under the law, in order to redeem those who were under the law, so that we might receive adoption as children" (Gal. 4:4-5). God's waiting affects us, and frequently we interpret it as inaction on the part of the Creator to whom we cry out. Dealing with feelings generated by the sense that nothing is happening, that God has forgotten us, is an important part of our growth as people of faith.

The Psalms are full of allusions to waiting and offer us a way to pray the distress (waiting for) as well as the trust (waiting with) that we feel as we live in the between times of unfulfilled hope. When life is consumed with problems or our bodies are pain-racked, we may not have words to express our prayers. The Psalms then can give voice to our longing:

> I will cry aloud to God;
>   I will cry aloud, and he will hear me.
> In the day of my trouble I sought the Lord;
>   my hands were stretched out by night and did not tire;
> I refused to be comforted.
>
> . . . .
>
> Has God forgotten to be gracious?
>   has he, in his anger, withheld his compassion?
> —*Psalm 77:1-2, 9* (BCP)

These are real prayers uttered by those who are overwhelmed by the badness of life and the perceived nonanswers of God.

The Babylonian exile of the Hebrew people gives rise to many of the Psalms that question God. Asaph, the author of Psalm 74, asks whether the Almighty has abandoned the covenant people forever and reminds God that not only is the chosen nation endangered by exile but also that God's stature in the world is brought into question. Psalms 74 and 80 picture God as the Shepherd of Israel. Asaph implies that God seems to remain angry with the sheep, unlike the caring shepherd who might use a staff to keep them together but does not continue to punish them. Asaph calls on God to remember, to take notice of suffering, and to see the enemy's devastation of the holy places in the land. He beseeches God, "Direct your steps to the perpetual ruins" (74:3). This seems to be more than an invitation for God to come and look at the destruction of the site where God and Israel convened. It is also a request that God trample and crush the enemy. In the past, prophets have been raised up and have offered signs of hope to God's people when they suffered oppression. Now Asaph can see no signs, and no prophets bring encouragement to the displaced people. He cries out in anguish, "How long, O God, is the foe to scoff? Is the enemy to revile your name forever?" (v. 10). The first eleven verses of this psalm reflect depression, despair, impotence, and a sense that life is a meaningless series of disasters.

The experience of exile is excruciatingly painful. To be cut off from one's roots, bereft of home and heritage, and compelled to exist in a foreign place is dreadfully lonely. I had a taste of this when I left my native England in 1981 and moved to the United States, where the Episcopal Church had agreed to test my vocation to the priesthood. I had loved my work teaching in a seminary but felt increasingly the call to ordained ministry. This was not an option for women in the Church of England. My self-imposed exile began with sadness at the loss of home, but it was also filled with hopeful anticipation as my ordination drew near. In the first months, I was busy planning the ordination service, adjusting to parish ministry, and enjoying the novelty of living in a new country. I was introduced to English muffins—I had never come across them in England—Jell-O salad, and new names for familiar vegetables like aubergines (eggplant) and courgettes (zucchini). American people hugged a lot more than the British (I liked that!) but they were far less direct, and I had to learn to hear "yes" or "no" in the politely wrapped responses to my questions. When my first temporary appointment came to an end, I moved to New York City to complete further graduate studies and to look for a new position. It was then, more than a year after I left England, that I began to experience a painful sense of loss and to feel that I did not belong in that teeming, vibrant, exciting, and tough city. With meager financial resources, no permanent parish appointment, and far from my friends in New Jersey, I felt lonely and dislocated.

I began to ask the "How long?" question of God and to question whether my decision to cross the Pond was really a choice made in response to an inner call. A faithful spiritual director helped me through this difficult period. I also found a good therapist. Neither of them offered me easy answers or a way to escape, but each provided support and the encouragement to be present to the disorientation. A dream also helped me to stay with the process and laugh at bit at myself. In the dream I was the producer of a play and, with my usual impatience, I wanted to get on with the rehearsal. All was chaos, with actors confused and milling around, so I turned to a group on my right and told them to take their places on stage. "But we are not ready yet, and we have forgotten our scripts," they replied. Frustrated, I turned to the group on my left, and they said, "We can't act our parts yet; they come much later in the play." The chaos continued as a small goat walked on stage, and I heard someone behind me say, "Pay attention to the goat; she is a very talented actress."

At the time, I was taking a course on dream work and recalled that we are not simply observers of our dreams but also participants in them. It didn't take me long to understand that my life did feel chaotic and that, like the group on my right, I had not yet "learned the lines" since I was a newbie Brit in the United States. And like the actors on the left, my time had not yet come. Stay in the uncertainty of chaotic experience and wait for the right time to "get this show on the road" seemed to be the message of the dream. But then there was the goat. Of course, I was also the goat, and a small one at that! Given the huge learning curve ahead of me I felt invisible. But then I remembered the voice. At a time when I was feeling inept, lacking adult skills to maneuver my way through a new church and country, the voice told me to pay attention to the goat—to the little kid within—and to trust that she had talents that would be used in their time. I was also able to laugh when I considered that the present situation was "getting my goat," but I heard very clearly God's invitation to wait and trust.

Waiting with God

THE PSALMS ALSO PUT US in touch with an attitude of waiting with God in childlike trust, even in adverse circumstances. Psalms 38-39 record David's suffering from a debilitating sickness and Psalm 40 expresses thanksgiving following deliverance from it.

I waited patiently for the LORD;
    he inclined to me and heard my cry.
He drew me up from the desolate pit,
    out of the miry bog,
and set my feet upon a rock (Ps. 40:1-2).

David saw his illness as a watery grave that threatened to swallow him alive even as the Red Sea had swallowed the Egyptians. He felt he was sinking in the clay, the very substance with which the oppressed Israelites were compelled to manufacture bricks. Now God had "firmed" his steps, enabled him to stand securely on a rock. David extends the song beyond his personal experience of healing to a communal celebration that speaks to the "waiting with God" that we all experience.

Waiting patiently with God becomes possible as we tune in to the Word of God, who addresses us in our need. David gives thanks that God gave him an "open ear" (v. 6), a listening that enabled him to refuse the insidious messages of discouragement. One morning I reflected on the appointed psalm in the Book of Common Prayer and the repeated antiphon addressed me: "The LORD of hosts is with us; the God of Jacob is our stronghold" (Ps. 46:4, 8, BCP). I was glad to claim the reassurance of the ancient Hebrew psalm and to take it into a day filled with thorny decisions and several meetings. I received the verse as a gift, repeated it thankfully, and allowed it to become my prayer. Then, as I sat in silence, I became aware of another persistent voice in the background repeating an old discouraging message. The message was familiar: life is fragile, the present moment insecure, and the future unpredictable. I tuned out the psalm and soon was experiencing anxiety as fear replaced confidence in God my Stronghold. But, graciously, God opened my ear again. With clarity I knew I had a choice about which voice I listened to. The old, worn-out, and fearful message was lifted from the unconscious, and I heard its shrill emptiness. I chose the psalm voice for the day.

David was able to tune out the voice of fear. As he did so, he heard once again the truth about God and himself. In this knowledge, no external circumstances could shake his confidence or shatter his faith, for nothing could rob him of the reality of God's truth within. It became possible to wait. Daring to journey within and to discover the word of God engraved deeply in our hearts means life. Other voices, some originating in childhood, may tell us that God's will means loss, endless waiting, and a denial of our deepest longings. Such lies keep us from fullness of life and the joy that comes from discovering that in the deepest part of ourselves we are at one with the Creator in what we truly desire. To wait with and on such a God is to find oneself in harmony with the cosmos, which is ever waiting, ever coming to fullness. Our waiting announces to the world that the God who waits is Creator of all times and seasons and gives meaning to the waiting times of our experience.

SUGGESTIONS FOR REFLECTION ~

What are you waiting for? Is there some desire that you have brought often to God, who seems not to respond? In your journal, begin an honest dialogue with God that expresses your longings and the anger or disappointment you feel. At the conclusion of your writing, ask yourself if there has been any shift in your feelings, any new insights.

PSALM PRAYER
> O God, sometimes I think you have forgotten me;
> sometimes my faith becomes very small.
> Please remind me that you have not abandoned me,
> for your faithfulness never changes.
> Help me to wait with patience
> and to trust that all time is in your hand.

WRITING A PSALM ~

Do you remember times when you have been disappointed in or angry with God? If so, how did you deal with those experiences? Is there something today that needs to be expressed but that you have kept hidden because you felt that you could not be truly honest about your feelings? Make a list of any memories that come to mind. Choose one incident to begin with and make it the opening sentence of your psalm. You do not need to censor your writing!

SIX

Celebrating
Creation

The heavens are telling the glory of God.

Psalm 19:1

THE PRAISE AND WORSHIP of God in the Psalms is predicated on the understanding that the God of the Hebrew people is also the Creator of everything that is. We all belong! The first "book" the Creator gave to humanity is revealed in the awesome unfolding of nature from darkness into light and in the gift of water, plants, animals, and humankind. Genesis 1 offers a glorious picture of God bringing the earth into being and seeing that it was good. When the first humans are created on the sixth day God notes that it was "*very* good" (v. 31, emphasis added). We need to return to this story often, especially if we find ourselves in a tradition that has neglected Genesis 1 in favor of the story in Genesis 3 with its emphasis on sin and separation from God. Indeed, we all stray away from the Divine, hiding ourselves guiltily in the bushes; but God is always seeking us out and restoring us to fellowship so that once again the Creator can see that it is "very good."

Nature makes visible the presence of God, and it is incumbent upon us, the people of God, to celebrate the wonders of creation and to give thanks. We spoke earlier of Psalm 19, which begins with the understanding that the heavens tell of God's glory. Nature is like a book that speaks to us when we take time to listen. Psalm 19 also celebrates the scriptures, that other book, which teaches us how to live. The Psalms were written in a largely rural environment, so we find frequent references to landscape, animals, birds, and plants throughout the Psalter.

> The earth is the LORD's and all that is in it,
>   the world, and those who live in it;
> for he has founded it on the seas,
>   and established it on the rivers.
> —*Psalm 24:1-2*

God is the Maker of all. Nothing lies outside God's creativity and care. We can see and hear God in every place.

My mother was a great lover of nature who turned our tiny backyard into a place of beauty. The yard was no more than a ten-foot concrete square, but with plant pots of many sizes filled with a variety of ferns and flowers, it spoke of her love of creation and the Creator. Hanging baskets draped on the crisscross fence were filled with creeping ivy and blooming flowers that brightened this little urban oasis. Some of the plants came from my grandmother's garden, and some were surreptitiously acquired from the woodlands where we often went for walks. As a teenager I could not really understand my mother's passion for nature and her acute pain at the suffering of any creature, even the earthworms that strayed from the soil to a frequently trodden path. She would rescue any creature in danger, and when she discovered in the woods a snare designed to catch rabbits, she returned home for wire cutters and tore it to shreds—several times. Because I followed my church's emphasis on the fundamental importance of the Bible as the only means of God's revelation and salvation, my mother's awareness of God in creation did not make sense to me. It was nice to have plants around, and I enjoyed our dog and cat; but I preferred reading reformist literature and studying the scriptures. I was unable to "hear" the God of all the earth speaking through all that had been created. It took years for me to receive the gift of passionate care for nature and the worship of God through creation that my mother held out to me.

Ancient World Pictures Still Speak to Us

PSALM 104 OFFERS a wonder-filled celebration of creation and shows the place of creatures, animal and human, in God's unfolding provision for all. The psalm begins by blessing God with an image of the Creator based on the observance of sky and earth. As the author gazes at the sky, he imagines God clothed in a garment of light and the sky stretched from horizon to horizon like a domed tent. The clouds that race across the sky are God's chariot, which the wind propels. The wind is a messenger of God to the earth, which sits firmly on foundations so that it cannot move or blow away. At the time of the psalmist, people believed that the earth was a flat disc supported by strong pillars and the domed sky above the world contained "windows" that opened at God's will to allow rain and snow to fall. Rain was perceived as a gift of God in times of drought but also spoke of God's displeasure when it was sent in the abundance that caused flooding. The overabundance of water at the beginning of creation became oceans and rivers at God's word once the dry land came into being: "'Let the waters under the sky be gathered together into one place, and let the dry land appear.' And it was so" (Gen. 1:9). Integrating the Creation story and the story of the Flood (Gen. 6:12–7:24), the author of Psalm 104 describes the waters standing above the mountains (vv. 6–9). At the rebuke of God, however, they fled to their proper place. God's word is all-powerful.

In our day, science has taught us so much more about the earth and its origins that we may be inclined to dismiss the poetic descriptions of the Hebrew writers. Yet similar poetic descriptions of nature persist in daily use. We still speak of sunrise and sunset despite our awareness that the sun does not move—we do! Who has not gazed on the glorious panorama of color ranging from pale yellow to deep vermilion at the beginning or end of the day and felt blessed by the experience?

We need the gift of imagination if we are to see and hear God in the world about us. Poetry, art, and music can take us to places that literal and scientific truth cannot. This is not to deny the importance of research and scholarship, but it invites us to reclaim the wisdom of our own creativity. I do not literally believe that God is "up there," racing across the sky in a convertible. But when I gaze reverently at the changes in the clouds moved by wind, I do lift my soul to the Creator. And sometimes, like Charlie Brown, I see some fantastical creatures in the clouds, and I giggle with delight because it seems that God has fun with creation. Why else would we see long-necked giraffes, elephants using their long noses to suck up water, camels with lumps on their backs, and so many other curious creatures?

Psalm 104 continues to unfold with a recital of all the creatures sustained by God. The streams that flow down from the hills provide drink for wild creatures, and the birds nest in nearby trees. Grass grows to feed cattle and plants flourish that we humans eat, including the produce of the grapevine and olive tree. The great cedars are God's planting, and on the mountains wild goats graze and rabbits build their burrows. Moon and sun have their place in the wonder of God's creativity as they mark the days and seasons. At night the big cats look for prey, but they hide away as the day returns and people go out to their work. Before the recital continues, the author finds himself so full of wonder that praise fills his being:

> O Lord, how manifold are your works!
>   In wisdom you have made them all;
>   the earth is full of your creatures.
> —*Psalm 104:24*

A sense of wonder is God's gift to us. Do we pause long enough to grasp the awesomeness of creation? I am blessed to live in the Blue Ridge Mountains of western North Carolina where every day I see something that delights my soul. I recall the young bear that walked up my path—for a moment I thought he was a large Labrador—and as he arrived at my pond, I startled him by yelling. He had one foot on the edge of a rock that wobbled and sent him headfirst into the water. When he came up for air, he sat in the pond and looked around in a daze as though he wondered what had happened to him! I look at the redbud tree planted three years ago that a well-meaning friend managed to flatten when turning his car in a snowstorm. It speaks to me of the tenacity and strength of creation, for it stands upright today and is a reminder of the grace of God that enables me to stand even when I have felt crushed. The mountains never fail to surprise me with their beauty no matter the weather. Sometimes they wear a snowcap above the orange and brown fall colors, and even in the rain they reveal a misty grace that tells of mystery. I have been in other places where it was a greater challenge to see the Creator in nature. For five years I lived in a tiny apartment in New York City and looked through window bars to see a small section of sky. While I was there it was the despised pigeons that blessed me as I watched them above a traffic signal, sitting calmly in a line while enraged cabdrivers yelled and screamed at each other in the gridlock below! I imagined them laughing together at the ludicrous behavior of humans! The grass forcing itself through the concrete sidewalk spoke to me of the awesome power of God, and walking in Central Park met my yearning for greenness as I bought pot plants to place on my windowsill. Nature is all around us; even in big cities the wind still blows, and day and night follow each other in an eternal rhythm that invites our gratitude.

When the psalmist returns to his reverie, the great sea with its many creatures catches his attention. The deeps include Leviathan (the whale) that God made to sport in the sea. The writers of the Talmud, an ancient text on Jewish law and tradition, suggest that God plays with the whales! "For three hours each day, God amuses Himself [sic] so to speak with Leviathan" (Avodah Zarah 3b).[1] What a glorious image! God needs playmates and so goes down into the deep oceans to swim and dance with the whales. This image is not to be taken literally, though who is to say that God does not reside in the oceans as well as the hills and deserts? Once again, here is a suggestion that we too can let our imagination be free to delight, like children, in the most amazing presence of God in all that God has made. Meditation on creation leads the writer to conclude the psalm with a song of praise: "May the glory of the LORD endure forever; may the LORD rejoice in his works.... I will sing to the LORD as long as I live; I will sing praise to my God while I have being. May my meditation be pleasing to [God].... Bless the LORD, O my soul. Praise the LORD!" (vv. 31, 33-35).

Caring for Creation

WE KNOW ONLY TOO WELL that today the earth is not as God created it to be. We see pollution of rivers, air, and oceans; decimation of hardwood forests; melting ice caps; and alarming climate changes. Does God still cry, "It is good!"? At the end of the Genesis 1 Creation story, God speaks to humankind, saying: "Prosper! Reproduce! Fill Earth! Take charge! Be responsible for fish in the sea and birds in the air, for every living thing that moves on the face of Earth" (Gen. 1:28, THE MESSAGE). In other words, God entrusts humanity with care of the earth and all that is in it. Many versions of the Bible translate this verse from the Hebrew as "have dominion over, " and sadly we have sometimes interpreted this as freedom to do with creation and creatures as we will. Rather than caring for creation, we have violated it, abused the creatures—human and animal—around us, and forgotten who we are as those created in the divine image to take responsibility on God's behalf. In his translation quoted above, Eugene Peterson reminds us of who we are and calls upon us to live responsively, caringly.

Stormy Passages

IT IS TEMPTING to acknowledge only the glorious, gentle, and won-der-filled aspects of nature and to deny the power of unleashed storms, tsunamis, earthquakes, and raging wildfires. The psalmists are realistic about creation, acknowledging that storms, earthquakes, and floods occur. They attribute these phenomena to God also. Psalm 107 vividly describes the terror of sailors caught in storms at sea.

[God] commanded and raised the stormy wind,
    which lifted up the waves of the sea.
They mounted up to heaven, they went down to the depths;
    their courage melted away in their calamity;
they reeled and staggered like drunkards,
    and were at their wits' end.
Then they cried to the LORD in their trouble,
    and he brought them out from their distress;
he made the storm be still,
    and the waves of the sea were hushed.
Then they were glad because they had quiet,
    and he brought them to their desired haven.
—*Psalm 107:25-30*

In the New Revised Standard Version Bible, Psalm 107 begins with the heading "Thanksgiving for Deliverance from Many Troubles," and it records the frequent struggles of God's people, especially during their years of journeying through the wilderness. The psalms of pain and suffering assure the people of God's deliverance when they turn from their sinful ways and cry out for help.

There have been a few times when I have been in physical danger. Once, two friends and I were hiking on a mountain in Wales during a whiteout. Foolishly we had not brought a compass and so had no idea where we were or where we should go. I cried out to God, "Help!" and we did find our way off the mountain safely. Another time I was with a group on board a Greek ferry returning to our cruise ship from one of the islands we had visited. We were packed tight, crowded together, hanging on wherever we could, and feeling nauseous as the small vessel navigated the choppy ocean. It was a dangerously over-crowded situation, but the cruise staff ignored safety issues because we were on the penultimate boat, and they wanted to make sure we all got back to the ship. Then there was the time I was driving home during rush hour after buying a car. Suddenly a van pulled out into the oncoming lane. Mercifully, there was a tiny turnout I was able to swerve into and so avoided a head-on crash by a split second. Unfortunately, the driver behind me had nowhere to go and bore the full force of the oncoming vehicle. These are examples of physical danger, but when I read the Psalms today, I read them less literally. Rather, I find in them many parallels to my journey through life.

On more than one occasion I have felt that "all your waves and your billows have gone over me" (Ps. 42:7) when some catastrophic event has occurred. Once, after working for a year developing a project in an academic institution, I fully expected to be hired to oversee the program that was now ready to be formally launched. In the large city, apartments were hard to find and I needed to make plans for the following year, so when the person in charge (who had become invisible lately) had said nothing to me, I went to see him. He left me standing on his doorstep after telling me that he had hired someone else to do the job because he questioned my stability. I was devastated, angry, and deeply disappointed that the work I had done seemed unappreciated. I felt overwhelmed, flooded with painful emotions, and knew I was powerless in that situation. The Psalms became my anchor, especially those that spoke of the experience of loss and betrayal.

Images of nature's turbulence provide metaphors for praying our disappointments instead of turning away from God and bottling up our anger or resentment. When we come to stormy passages, we can by God's grace reach out and find a hand beckoning us, just as Peter did on the Sea of Galilee when he began to sink in the waves (Matt. 14:28-33). The storm does not always stop at the moment we turn to God for help, but we are given the grace to remain in the disordered, painful place, now no longer feeling alone. The loss of a loved one—through death or some other circumstance—plunges us into a pit of pain. Grief needs time to heal, and learning to be patient with God and ourselves is important.

I waited patiently for the LORD;
he inclined to me and heard my cry.
He drew me up from the desolate pit,
out of the miry bog (Ps. 40:1-2).

Sometimes we just have to remain in the pit, trusting that God too stands in the mucky place. God holds us in the time of our sorrow and will journey out of the pit with us when we are ready.

The grief of loss never completely leaves us, but the God of storm and flood repeatedly lifts us up and gives us new hope.

Now my head is lifted up
    above my enemies all around me,
and I will offer in his tent
    sacrifices with shouts of joy.
—*Psalm 27:6*

Perhaps our greatest enemy is fear when hope seems hard to come by, but the God who is Creator of the cosmos rejoices with us in mountaintop moments and invites us to rest in the arms of compassion that embrace us in the darkest moments of our experience.

SUGGESTIONS FOR REFLECTION ∼

Find a leaf, flower, rock, or other natural object that you can hold. Take time simply to "be" with the object. Notice its color, texture, shape, and structure. Don't rush on to associate thoughts or ideas with it. When you have spent some minutes observing the object, allow your thoughts to wander. Is there a memory, image, scripture, or situation that comes to mind? There is no need to censor your thoughts. Next identify one memory, image, or idea and stay with it. Where do you sense that God is speaking to you? How will you respond to the invitation or challenge that God brings you? You may notice that this is a form of *lectio divina* that can be applied to objects.

PSALM PRAYER

O God of Creation, sometimes I want to dance with joy
when I see beauty in all that you have made.
Thank you for the sky, brilliant with color,
or covered with shafts of light through dark clouds.
Thank you for water that sustains us in life
and for earth that provides food and shelter.
Thank you for the air we breathe
and for fire that brings us warmth.
O God of Creation, keep calling us to care;
make us good stewards of the earth
so all may share its good resources
and pollution is no more.

WRITING A PSALM ∿

Your psalm may flow naturally from the suggested reflection on something of nature. Psalms can be descriptive and filled with wonder at
the micro and macro dimensions of creation. Consider writing your
response to the exercise in the form of a psalm and choosing a phrase
to use as a refrain. An example might be: "God of creation, we give
thanks for the earth."

SEVEN

Touching the Holy
in the Ordinary

The vineyard of the LORD of hosts...
Isaiah 5:7

NOT ALL THE PSALMS in the Hebrew scriptures are contained in the present book of Psalms. Some are encapsulated in stories of a character in Israel's life; some use imagery to represent the way in which Yahweh "sees" the people and calls upon them to live faithfully. Not all were written to be chanted antiphonally by large choirs. We find a good example in the case of Jonah, whose psalm occurs while he is inside a great fish.

> "I called to the LORD out of my distress,
>   and he answered me;
> out of the belly of Sheol I cried,
>   and you heard my voice.
>
> . . . .
>
> The waters closed in over me;
>   the deep surrounded me;
> weeds were wrapped around my head
>   at the roots of the mountains.
>
> . . . .

Those who worship vain idols
    forsake their true loyalty.
But I with the voice of thanksgiving
    will sacrifice to you;
what I have vowed I will pay,
    Deliverance belongs to the LORD!"
—*Jonah 2:2, 5, 8–9*

When the psalm ends, we read this succinct verse: "Then the LORD spoke to the fish, and it spewed Jonah out upon the dry land" (v. 10). We can only imagine the scene: a disobedient prophet now freed from his sticky, stinking prison, lying dazed on a beach in the land to which God had called him in the first place.

In times of great distress and in times of exquisite joy, the people of God give voice to their experience in song. The book of Jonah was likely written to challenge those who wanted to build an exclusionary "wall" around the Jewish people after they had returned from exile. Some who had been left behind when the Babylonians captured Jerusalem had intermarried. These Samaritans had adopted worship that, in the eyes of the religious leaders of Israel, was not pure. So along comes this delightful story about a rebellious prophet who had strong opinions concerning those who did not belong in Israel. It critiques the exclusionary position of the purists.

Jonah's story has relevance beyond its immediate context. It challenges us today to ask ourselves how welcoming and inclusive our communities are. When I look at Jonah, I find myself! Like him, I really want to do God's will, but when God challenges my opinion of how and where ministry must be done, I want to run from the demands. Jonah decided to board a ship going in the opposite direction from God's choice, and a great storm arose. The storm that threatened to break up the ship and drown everyone was perceived to be the result of disobedience. Jonah owned his guilt and offered to be thrown overboard so that the ship and its passengers might be spared. And there God has a great fish waiting! So for three days Jonah traveled inside the belly of the fish, which took him to the very place

God wanted him to be. Sometimes God uses very unconventional means to get us to the place of ministry!

Once in Nineveh, Jonah began to preach to the people he wanted to keep out of God's circle of belonging, but his success as a preacher did not make him happy. Jonah still did not want "those people" to be included. The psalm he composed while inside the great fish was soon forgotten once he landed. The book ends with the unhappy prophet pouting as he sits under a bush, which dries up after God "prepared a sultry east wind, and the sun beat down on the head of Jonah" (Jonah 4:8). The Hebrew writer did not tack on a "happy-ever-after" ending to the story but rather let it stand as a testimony to Jonah's, and our, reluctance to let go of prejudice and expand our vision of the realm of God. Many of us resist change in any form, but when it comes to widening our borders, it takes a long time to develop an attitude of inclusion and acceptance.

The story of Jonah reminds us that God is present in the ordinary and uses natural things to communicate holy Presence. It is very hard to outwit God, and perhaps Jonah's most intense prayer was the one he prayed in the belly of the fish. God used a bush burning in the desert to call the fugitive murderer Moses from sheepherding to leading God's people out of slavery (Exod. 3:1-10). Moses also came up with some excuses before he finally did what God asked of him (Exod. 3:11-13). At the top of Mount Horeb, wind, earthquake, and fire assailed Elijah as he fearfully fled from the wrath of Queen Jezebel. He did not hear God in these phenomena but rather in the quietness that followed, "a sound of sheer silence" (1 Kings 19:12). Jacob, fleeing from his father and brother, slept from exhaustion in the wilderness alone and far from the home he associated with the God of Israel. In the desert he dreamed of a ladder reaching from earth to heaven with angels passing up and down upon it and came to the realization, "Surely the LORD is in this place—and I did not know it!" (Gen. 28:16). The rock that had served as a pillow for Jacob he now set up as an altar and poured oil on it to signify his recognition of the awesomeness of the barren place he perceived as the house of God and the gate of heaven (Gen. 28:17-18). God becomes known to people where they are and uses what is before their eyes to convey divine truth.

Justice Close to Home

ANOTHER PSALM that lies outside the present collection is in Isaiah 5:1-30, where the prophet compares God's people to a vineyard that has failed to produce fruit:

> Let me sing for my beloved
>   my love-song concerning his vineyard:
> My beloved had a vineyard
>   on a very fertile hill.
> He dug it and cleared it of stones,
>   and planted it with choice vines;
> he built a watchtower in the midst of it,
>   and hewed out a wine vat in it;
> he expected it to yield grapes,
>   but it yielded wild grapes.
> —*Isaiah 5:1-2*

The first seven verses spell out the theme of the psalm, which addresses unfaithful Israel. The author emphasizes God's caring. The "beloved" selects a fertile area and undertakes the onerous task of ridding the ground of rocks. God then plants choice vines and makes every effort to protect the vineyard and prepare for harvest. But when God looks for fruitfulness there are only sour, wild grapes on the vines. The passage reflects the story of Adam and Eve in Genesis 3, where the human pair, in the wonderful garden that God had created, rebelled against their Creator.

God's generosity and care should have resulted in an abundant harvest, so God asks, "What more was there to do for my vineyard that I have not done in it?" (Isa. 5:4). The psalm goes on to say that the vineyard of the LORD of hosts is none other than Israel; it is

God's pleasant planting. God made clear to Israel the parameters for faithful living and expected justice but found only bloodshed, desired righteousness but heard cries of anguish. This psalm is a summons to repentance and the faithfulness to which God calls the people. It stands as an invitation to examine our lives: Where might our faithfulness to the word of God be lacking? How do we relate to one another as the covenant community? Are we fruitful in our commitment to spiritual disciplines and in our outreach to those in need? Are we expecting to hear God speak to us in the ordinary things about us, or do we think we will find God's way only through sermons?

When I led a church group on a pilgrimage to South Africa, we enjoyed the beauty of the land and saw up close the flora and fauna of the country. We saw succulent desert plants, colorful blooms in the bush, flaming aloe, and the variety of colors of the protea, South Africa's national flower. We visited game reserves where we came into close contact with animals large and small: a herd of elephants surrounded our vehicle, and we watched the small dung beetles scuttling across the dirt road pushing mounds of animal droppings before them. But the most impressive experience happened when we visited the townships, where people lived in deep poverty. Endless rows of decrepit shacks had greeted us along the highway when we left the Cape Town airport. Shocking as that was, it could not compare to being among the people who lived in these "homes." We went to a Methodist church where children arrived when school was over to receive the only meal of the day—a hunk of pot bread and a bowl of soup or stew made with whatever was available. It was easy to see that in post-apartheid South Africa, injustice and poverty were still realities. The challenge for us, however, was to look at our ministry back home and to ask ourselves where the poor were to be found.

Out of the pilgrimage experience came the suggestion that our church begin a food pantry since other local organizations offered advice, clothing, and funds to assist with such needs as rent and heating. The first week a handful of people came, but today between 350 and 425 people can get basic groceries for a week. Because the economy has been in a downturn, many of our clients are the working poor, including single parents who sometimes work two or more jobs but still do not make enough money to care adequately for their children. God did not criticize the people of Israel because they did not worship the right way or believe the right things but because they did not act justly, failing to hear the cries of the oppressed. The "fruit" God expected was not smiling faces on Sunday mornings (though I am sure God was glad to see people worshiping and greeting one another). God longed much more to see the covenant community expanding its borders to include all people, especially the needy.

Delighting in God

THE LITTLE BOOK of the prophet Habakkuk is written almost entirely in psalm form. The skeptical prophet writes to address the oppression of God's people and to ask the question, "How can a just God allow ongoing oppression by the wicked?" There is some debate among scholars about the date of the book and the possibility that Habakkuk is using earlier sources, but his message fits the Greek period about 331 BCE. The first chapter contains Habakkuk's complaint about the injustice that continues to dominate the Jewish people. Then God responds by telling the prophet to write a vision of hope that predicts an end to the present suffering (Hab. 2:2-3). A description follows of the woes and punishment of the wicked. Then in chapter 3, Habakkuk offers a prayer in which he reminds God of grace received in times past. "Please do it again!" he cries to the God of salvation who is visible in the cataclysms of nature and the defeat of enemies.

In many ways Habakkuk offers a recitation similar to the psalms in which the writers call on God to act once again after reminding the Creator how the people have been delivered in the past. The last three verses of the book are a surprise. They point us to the remarkable truth that trust and even delight can become the song of those who do not serve God only when their prayers are answered:

Though the fig tree does not blossom,
   and no fruit is on the vines;
though the produce of the olive fails,
   and the fields yield no food;
though the flock is cut off from the fold,
   and there is no herd in the stalls,
yet I will rejoice in the LORD;
   I will exult in the God of my salvation.
GOD the Lord, is my strength;
   he makes my feet like the feet of a deer,
   and makes me tread upon the heights.
—*Habakkuk 3:17-19*

I grew up in a tradition where it was common for believers to give testimonies about their experience of God, and often we were encouraged by their stories. I remember one young woman who told of God's grace when she ran into a busy street to end her life and, miraculously, the car missed her. At this crucial point in her life, she realized that God had not wanted her to die but to come to faith. I heard other dramatic stories, and I was always a bit chagrined that I never had a dramatic conversion experience to relate! Later, when I was serving a church in Manhattan, we had a mission weekend in which visiting Christians shared their faith in order to encourage us to deeper commitment to Christ. On Sunday the speaker preached about his own life at a time when his marriage was falling apart, his business was on the brink of bankruptcy, and one of his children with alcohol and drug addictions had run away from home. He spoke eloquently about the pain and despair he felt until a Christian friend invited him to church, where he experienced a life-changing conversion. The man told us with great joy that following his conversion, he and his wife entered counseling and saved their marriage; his business turned around and was now growing rapidly; and the teenage child had agreed to enter a rehabilitation program. He praised God for all the blessings he had received.

At one level I rejoiced with this man in his experience of transformation, but a niggling thought kept playing in my mind. *What would his testimony have been if his marriage had ended in divorce, his business in bankruptcy, and his child living on the streets?* In such extreme circumstances, would he still have been giving thanks to God and dancing like Habakkuk? The prophet relates a worst-case scenario in which none of his dreams and hopes is realized, but then he goes on to say "yet." So much rests on that little word. "Yet I will rejoice in the LORD." My faith will not be shaken, and my hope will not be lost. In the Christian scriptures, we find many examples of confidence in God during outward disaster. Stephen, the first Christian martyr, kept before him the vision of Christ in glory and prayed for his persecutors as they stoned him to death (Acts 7:60). Paul and Silas—arrested, flogged, and shackled in a dark interior prison cell—prayed and sang praises to God, and other prisoners heard them. The two missionaries were miraculously freed when an earthquake struck the prison but *their trust and thanksgiving preceded their release* (Acts 16:16-40).

Learning to rejoice like Habakkuk requires trust and the knowledge that God is not distant but intimately present with us moment by moment. In light of Christian faith, we celebrate Jesus' promises to his disciples and "those who will believe in me through their word" (John 17:20). That includes us. In chapters 14–17 of the Gospel according to Saint John, Jesus makes it clear that his end is near. Nevertheless, he promises that he will prepare a place for followers and that the Spirit, who has been with them while he was alive, will be in them in a yet more intimate way. On the day of Pentecost, in a dramatic way the Holy Spirit came upon the followers of Jesus who were hiding in an upstairs room in Jerusalem and transformed them into bold witnesses of the good news in Jesus. The Spirit energizes, enables, leads, and encourages all who put their trust in Christ, whether times are very good or incredibly bad. We have more reason than Habakkuk to say,

> I'm singing joyful praise to GOD.
> I'm turning cartwheels of joy to my Savior God.
> Counting on GOD's Rule to prevail,

I take heart and gain strength.
I run like a deer.
I feel like I'm king of the mountain!
—*Habakkuk. 3:18-19* (THE MESSAGE)

Pain, loss, and suffering inevitably come our way. It is inappropriate to deny these realities, but deep within our being lies the assurance that God has not abandoned us, and whatever the outcome, we can trust in God's promises.

SUGGESTIONS FOR REFLECTION 〜

Paul writes to the Christians in Rome:

We are more than conquerors through him who loved us. For I am convinced that neither death, nor life, nor angels, nor rulers, nor things present, nor things to come, nor powers, nor height, nor depth, nor anything else in all creation, will be able to separate us from the love of God in Christ Jesus our Lord (Rom. 8:37–39).

Take some time to ponder this powerful statement of faith. When have you doubted your ability to trust God again? Journaling your answer may be helpful. You might also choose to hold in prayer anyone known to you who is suffering deeply and needs to feel upheld in a devastating time.

PSALM PRAYER
O God, come to meet me
in ocean depth and on the mountaintop.
Thank you for tending my life
like a faithful gardener.
Help me to be fruitful in trust
and patient in adversity.
Your blessing brings me joy,
and I want to dance in your presence forever.

WRITING A PSALM ∽

Ordinary moments and objects are sometimes transformed for us because we sense God's presence in them. God has always been present, but it takes silence and reflection time to recognize holy Presence. And sometimes the Creator breaks through our numbness to reveal Godself in surprising ways. Identify such moments in your experience and let one or more of the images become the focus of your psalm.

EIGHT

Discovering Joy
and Learning to Praise

Praise [God] with trumpet sound.
Psalm 150:3

PRAISE OF GOD is the vocation of all creation and is especially incumbent on humankind. We are capable of awareness that the Creator is our ultimate authority and has given us instruction on how to live. To our Creator we owe gratitude and thanksgiving for all the blessings we enjoy. Praise weaves its way through the Psalms and sometimes expresses itself as an act of faith when things are not going well. Psalm 51 is identified as David's song, offered out of deep penitence following his adultery with Bathsheba and the murder of her husband, Uriah. David pleads for mercy and forgiveness and prays that God will open his guilty lips to sing praise once again. Verse 15 has become the opening sentence of many liturgical forms of morning prayer: "O Lord, open my lips, and my mouth will declare your praise." The Psalms are a form of response to the awesomeness of the Creator, a recognition of God's action in the individual, community, and cosmos. And praise frequently is accompanied by dance and musical instruments, including trumpet, ram's horn, lyre, harp, timbrel, pipe, strings, and cymbals (Ps. 150, BCP). The kind of praise we see in ancient Israel is, according to Walter Brueggemann, a means of maintaining and transforming the world as well as receiving God's blessings.[1]

In my tradition, the Episcopal Church, the liturgy is reverent, ordered, and eucharistic, involving the music of a fine organ and the voices of a choir. Singing by the rest of the congregation can be sparse at times! We always include psalms in our worship, and some of us have even learned how to chant these ancient songs. Occasionally, the presence of a flute player, harpist, or cellist blesses us, and at major festivals a trio of brass instruments augments worship. I deeply appreciate the order and predictability of the service, but it is a joyful experience to be among my United Methodist friends at the Academy for Spiritual Formation, where the singing is full-throated, enthusiastic, and accompanied by a variety of instruments.[2] This kind of music sets me free and makes me want to dance.

We need a balance in our worship and a wider experience of the people of God coming together to offer praise. Many years ago in England, I co-led a weekend liturgical dance workshop in a convent of rather serious nuns. The workshop was not held for the community, but one of the sisters in her eighties opted to join us. She put her whole body into the movement and clearly felt a freedom to praise God in an entirely new way. The Sunday Eucharist included a gathering together of the dances we had learned, accompanied by tambourines, rain sticks, rattles, and wind instruments. We closed with a circle dance after which lunch was to be served, but the sister was not ready for the dance to end. She took up a tambourine, cried, "Follow me," and led us in a wild, high-kicking, snakelike dance, which finally ended in the dining room. Praise of God is liberating and transformative.

Once a year in my church the whole community joins in procession around the church. On Palm Sunday, we read the Gospel story of Jesus riding into Jerusalem as the crowd throws palms and garments in the road and shouts its recognition of Christ as the Son of David, the Messiah. Instead of the orderly procession of choir, acolytes, and clergy, everyone processes out of the pews and for a single day experiences the embodiment of praise. I wonder how our worship might be transformed if we identified other occasions for the community to journey together outside the safety of a pew. One of the reasons I love to lead pilgrimages is because the people bless me as we travel together. Sometimes the journey is uncomfortable in a crowded aircraft; sometimes a ferry, car, or bus conveys us; and often we need to travel on foot. Our group goes to sacred places where we honor those who have gone before us on the pilgrimage of faith, but often the transformative moments occur as we tell stories, rub up against one another, and share discomfort as well as joy. That is the way the Hebrew people became a community through long years of wandering in wilderness places and then through a history of defeat by Assyrian, Babylonian, and Persian empires. Even when they could reclaim Jerusalem and the Temple, it was under Roman rule. They sang their way through exile and restoration using the psalms that sustained their forbears.

Praise Is God's Due

PSALM 65 OPENS with these words: "Praise is due to you, O God, in Zion; and to you shall vows be performed." The context of the psalm is a three-year famine and the threat of enemies. Jewish tradition attributes the psalm to David, who has learned not only to cry to God for help but always to offer God praise. In times of great hardship, the people are to remember the awesomeness of God's deeds, the wonder of God's power over creation, and the abundant harvest God has brought to pass in previous years. The psalm ends with an expression of hope in the restoration of the harvest, a hope in which the very creation expresses joy:

> The pastures of the wilderness overflow,
>   the hills gird themselves with joy,
> the meadows clothe themselves with flocks,
>   the valleys deck themselves with grain,
> they shout and sing together for joy.
> —*Psalm 65:12–13*

The Very Creation Praises God

THE OBLIGATION TO PRAISE GOD appears in many of our hymns, which are analogous to the Psalms.[3] Praise is not simply a response to what is good when we are inclined to be thankful but a moment-by-moment attitude of gratefulness that honors God for our very being as individuals and as a community. I wrote earlier of my struggles related to the sudden closure of the monastery I had called home for several years. When I am in a place of disappointment and pain, my inclination is to go into the natural world (after I have allowed my anger to become self-pity for a while). I am not by nature a Pollyanna kind of person who makes lemonade out of lemons; a bit of shouting, moaning, and giving way to fear is usually my first reaction to loss. Nature is the most healing and grounding place for me. There I am able to see a picture bigger than the one visible to the myopic loss of vision in times of stress. So, even on a foggy day beside an invisible ocean, grace reminds me that God is to be praised and that there have been many other times when I have received deliverance from the fear of uncertainty and change. Praise begins to emerge in thanksgiving for the blessings of the past, and praise calls to mind that God and not my agitated self is in charge. Sometimes I imagine that the trees are dancing, the grass is returning to the dry earth, and the birds who sing in every season are praising God on my behalf.

According to Hebrew commentary, Psalm 71 describes David as in "old age and gray hairs" (v. 18) fleeing from his son Absalom.[4] When David ran from Saul in his youth, he had been sustained by hope and the sense of invincibility that often accompanies us in our younger days. Now, as an old man, the specter of death lies before him. He fears that he might not live long enough to regain his crown. David cries out to God and remembers that God has sustained him since his birth: "Upon you I have leaned from my birth; it was you who took me from my mother's womb. My praise is continually of you" (v. 6). Within the ongoing recital of the difficulties that surround him and the people who mock him, David does not forget praise; we sense in the psalm a gradual letting go of fear. He is willing to wait patiently for God to act and says that he will praise God more and more and recount God's mighty acts and saving deeds. Remembering God's goodness in the past leads to the reassurance that "You who have made me see many troubles and calamities will revive me again; from the depths of the earth you will bring me up again" (v. 20). We not only need to tell our stories to one another for mutual support and encouragement but also to tell them to ourselves as David seems to do here, especially in times when it is hard to praise God. The word *remember* appears constantly in the Hebrew scriptures, perhaps because, like us, God's ancient people all too soon forgot the blessings of the past and their need to praise God.

Everything That Has Breath

THE LAST FEW PSALMS in the Psalter take praise to the highest level and call the whole cosmos to praise the Creator. Psalm 148 names those who are to praise God: angels and the host of heaven, sun, moon, sea-monsters, hail, snow, fog, wind, mountains, hills, fruit trees, cedars, cattle, creeping things, birds, kings, and all people (BCP). Here there is no separation between humans and all else in creation; praise of God is the purpose of all creation.

As I read this psalm again, I noticed for the first time the inclusion of fog in the list and thank God for the fogs that have taught me to wait with hope. Today we have a growing concern for the earth, which has been polluted, abused, and destroyed in many places by human action. The rivers, called to praise God, run with toxic waste that kills fish and renders the water unsafe to drink. Ancient forests are torn down for timber and to make roads through areas that have provided habitat for creatures now in decline. Landfills are overflowing with waste that will not decompose, the ozone layer is permeable, and those who eat high on the food chain deny adequate nutrition to the poor. And we begin to care. We are concerned that the earth's resources are at risk, and we take action to alert governments and organizations to the disaster that is likely if we do not change. But the psalmists have a more profound view of the earth. We must act so that everything can fulfill its rightful place by praising God as God is entitled to be praised. There are no exceptions.

The last psalm, 150, begins with a great "Hallelujah!" and calls upon us to praise God in the temple *and* in the firmament of God's power (BCP). We naturally think of our places of worship as the location of God's praise, but we may forget that outside, where the protection of buildings is absent, God also wants our praise. Much of Israel's worship took place outside any temple or synagogue. During the wilderness years, they constructed a tent in which God could dwell, but the people stood outside to worship. Many processions led the community to Jerusalem, the people singing psalms as they traveled beside rivers, through deserts, and over mountainous terrain. Nature was always with them.

Psalm 24 may be a recitation of the experience of pilgrimage and the cry of the people as they came to the gates of Jerusalem, the destiny of their journey. They have traveled with the awareness that the whole earth belongs to God and that the "hill of the LORD" can be ascended only by those who have "clean hands and pure hearts" (vv. 3-4, BCP). In other words, how they live—faithful to the Torah—is important if they are to receive God's blessing and enter the Holy City. They call upon the watchman to open the gates and are required to repeat their request, declaring that the King of glory, who is also the LORD of hosts, awaits entrance. The people of God did not live with the sense of separation between nature and themselves; and here they do not consider that their God relates only to a chosen people. They worship the Creator God, the ultimate deity who made all things to give praise.

Psalm 150, in a sense, summarizes the entire book. The Psalms were composed to give God's people an opportunity to develop and enrich their souls by recognizing and offering praise for all the accomplishments and kindnesses of God. One of the challenges they faced, and we with them, was to learn to recognize God in every situation. The Psalms assist us in this process and offer us words to express our experience even when we do not have words of our own.

In tranquil, blissful times, we naturally praise God; but when life becomes turbulent and we are disoriented, a different opportunity for praise arises. The instruments named in this psalm represent the variety of moods we encounter. The strong blast of the shofar (ram's horn) causes people to tremble, overwhelmed by the awareness of their unrighteous behavior before Yahweh. The lyre and harp have a more gentle sound and call for praise that life also offers wonderfully tranquil times when we can rest in God's embrace. And all too often the rush and turbulence of life pummels us like the fast tempo of the cymbal. Then it is important to remember to praise God. The psalm ends as it began with "Hallelujah!"[5]

What a wondrous gift Love wrapped for us in the book of Psalms. My monastery years reinforced the blessing of having remembered access to a psalm I needed for a particular experience. I miss the bell calling me to prayer. I miss singing the Psalter five times a day. But recently God has given me another gift. I live about a mile from a railroad line that runs through town, and there are three crossings within a short distance of one another. I started noticing the trains and praying for those who drove them, and now the blast of the warning siren has become a "bell" for me. It reminds me to stop what I am doing, turn to God in prayer, and allow praise to intercept the sometimes mundane moments of my day. And the Psalms are right at hand to assist me with my own hallelujahs!

SUGGESTIONS FOR REFLECTION ∼

In your journal, list some experiences of the past week for which you give praise and thanks to God. If possible, sit or stand outside and observe the ways in which nature praises God. What does it mean to you to be "rooted and grounded in love" (Eph. 3:17)?

PSALM PRAYER

> God, your praise rings out in all the earth, in all your creatures;
> remind me to praise you often.
> I praise you as I awaken to a new day

and praise you when night falls.
I am created in your image, created for praise.
Let me live from the fullness of my humanity,
The pesky squirrel, the sleeping cat, and the ancient oak
express their praise by being themselves.
So may my praise come from my being
to you the God of the planets.
God of grace, praise belongs to you;
let me never forget to give you what is yours.
Hallelujah.

WRITING A PSALM ∾

By now you are familiar with the psalm-writing process. As you come to the end of this book, recall what has brought you joy in your present experience and on your life journey. Create a praise psalm naming as many causes for praise as you can. If there are too many, think about grouping them together in categories. And please keep on writing psalms!

NOTES ∾

CHAPTER 1

1. Nan C. Merrill, *Psalms for Praying: An Invitation to Wholeness*, 10th Anniversary Edition (New York: Continuum International, 2006).

CHAPTER 2

1. Saint Symeon the New Theologian, *Hymns of Divine Love*, trans. George A. Maloney (Denville, NJ: Dimension Books, 1976), 54.

2. A mantra is a short phrase or word repeated to facilitate quiet reflection and lead to transformation. This model of prayer has been practiced in the Christian church since at least the fourth century CE when the Jesus Prayer was recited by those trying to bring their thoughts into captivity to Christ. The short form of the Jesus Prayer is "Lord Jesus Christ, have mercy on me." It provides a wonderful rhythm for walking prayer. The word *mantra* comes from the Vedic tradition within Hinduism, but its Christian usage is specifically oriented toward reflection on scripture.

3. Taizé is a village in the Burgundy region of France and the site of an ecumenical community founded by Brother Roger. Young people from around the world gather to learn, study, and worship together. The liturgy is simple; short readings from scripture, silence, and chanting form the service, and icons are set up in various parts of the worship space. There are no chairs; people sit on the floor or use prayer benches. For more information and to find CDs of Taizé chants go to info@Taize.fr.

88 FINDING YOUR VOICE IN THE PSALMS

CHAPTER 3

1. From "Count Your Blessings," words and music by Burl Ives on the album *I Do Believe*, Word ST 91423 (Waco, Tex.: Word Records, Inc., 1967).

2. Wayne Muller, *Sabbath: Finding Rest, Renewal, and Delight in Our Busy Lives* (New York: Bantam Books, 1999), 27.

CHAPTER 6

1. Rabbis Nosson Scherman and Meir Zlotwitz, eds. *Tehillim*, vol. 2 (New York: Mesorah Publications, 1977), 1264i.

CHAPTER 8

1. Walter Brueggemann *Israel's Praise: Doxology against Idolatry and Ideology* (Philadelphia: Fortress Press, 1988), 11.

2. I have been blessed to serve on the faculty at many sessions of the Academy for Spiritual Formation offered by The Upper Room. The two-year program offers many of the disciplines named in this book. For more information go to: www.upperroom.org and click on programs.

3. Fourteen hymns begin with the word *Praise* in the hymnal of the Episcopal Church, and many more incorporate the praise of God into the body of the hymn.

4. Rabbis Nosson Scherman and Meir Zlotwitz, eds., *Tehillim*, vol. 1 (New York: Mesorah Publications, 1977), 877.

5. The names of the instruments given here are from the Book of Common Prayer translation.

A GUIDE FOR GROUP CONVERSATION
AND PRAYER ～

WHILE THIS BOOK is designed to be read by individuals and offers suggestions for personal reflection, it is also appropriate for group study in a church-related or ecumenical setting. The group facilitator does not need to be a clergy person, but some skills in group leadership will help the process to be inclusive and faithful to the practices outlined in the introduction.

An eight-week course of study is ideal. Ask participants to commit to the whole program so that the group can foster an atmosphere of trust and confidentiality. Ninety minutes will allow time to enter into silence, pay attention to a psalm, engage in personal writing of contemporary psalms based on the theme of the week, and share writing. Ask participants to sign up for the group and to acquire the book (or offer to order it for them). They should read the introduction and chapters 1 and 2 before attending the first meeting.

Preparation for the Meetings

As THE FACILITATOR, plan to oversee the setup of the meeting place and to arrive before the participants. Hospitality, a key element in planning, includes attention to lighting, comfortable seating, adequate warmth or coolness, and access to drinking water. You may choose to supply other beverages, but remember this is not a social gathering.

Invite participants to enter quietly into the space. Soft music will create an appropriate atmosphere as people arrive, and a candle burning in the center of the room, or other inviting symbols, may be used.

In preparing to facilitate the group's interaction, be cautious not to lose sight of your meeting's purpose: learning to pray with the Psalms and to write new psalms. It's easy for time together to be overtaken by too much talking. Also, as leader, you may need to suggest gently that each person receive equal time, especially if someone tends to dominate the group. Consider using a baton or other object as a "talking stick" that is passed to the speaker with the understanding that she or he is the only one who has the floor at that time.

As indicated above, ask participants to read the introduction and chapters 1 and 2 before arriving at the meeting. The structure and time of each meeting is based on 90 minutes.

Week 1

Welcome (5 minutes)
This first gathering will set the tone for the entire course, so it is important to help each person feel welcome and reassured that no one will be compelled to speak or share before being ready to do so. Explain that each gathering will include simple exercises, quiet time, opportunities to share insights, and time to compose psalms. If you wish, you may provide each person with a notebook that can be used as a prayer/psalm journal.

Beginning (10 minutes)
To begin the time, invite participants to join you in the model for praying Psalm 46:10 offered on page 30 and let them know that a period of silence will follow.

Engaging (30 minutes)
Following the brief silence, invite participants to say a few words about themselves and to comment on why they are attracted to the

Psalms—or turned off by them! What do they hope to receive from their commitment to this course? Next invite conversation about the chapters assigned for the week by posing questions such as: What in this chapter resonated with your own experience? What helps you to be still in God's presence? What are your challenges with this kind of prayer?

Practicing (20 minutes)

Remind the group of the model of *lectio divina* outlined in chapter 1 of the book. Explain the purpose of the four stages: *lectio* (reading), *ruminatio* (meditation), *oratio* (response), and *contemplatio* (contemplation), and assure participants that often the process is not as neat and orderly in practice. Tell them that you are about to introduce a group form of *lectio divina* to help everyone get started with the model.

Hand out a copy of Psalm 40:1-3 to each person and ask for three readers. Follow the model offered in chapter 1, but instead of having people respond aloud to each of the questions, ask them to write down the word or phrase that speaks to them, the place where the passage touches their lives, and the response it is calling them to make in the coming week. End with a time of silent prayer. Next invite any who are willing to do so to share their experience of this form of *lectio divina*.

Writing (20 minutes)

The last part of the session is given to writing individual psalms and sharing them with the group. Allow twenty minutes for the writing and a further five minutes for the closing, when people read the psalms they have written. First, remind the group of their assignment for next week (reading and practicing chapter 3).

Closing (5 minutes)

You may wish to stand or sit in a circle for the closing. The leader can conclude with a prepared prayer or spontaneous expression of thanks to God. An alternative ending might be to use an abbreviated form of the liturgy for evening prayer in *The Upper Room Worshipbook*, or other resource.

Week 2

Beginning (10 minutes)
Be sure the meeting space has been prepared appropriately. Welcome group members to this second meeting. Then begin the session with "Be still, and know that I am God" again or choose a simple chant such as "Wait for the Lord" found in *The Upper Room Worshipbook* (No. 396).

Engaging (30 minutes)
In place of introductions, invite the group to respond to questions such as, What has been the highlight for you as you continued to work with the Psalms this past week? What questions have emerged? How is your journal shaping up?

Practicing (20 minutes)
This week enter into group *lectio divina* by following the order on page 16, but first tell participants that this time they will be invited to speak their responses following the three readings. Again, make sure they know that it is acceptable to pass and let them know that at the end, the group will pray around a circle. This will make it important to listen carefully to what others are saying, especially the person on your right. Choose an appropriate psalm and make sure everyone has a copy. At the end, invite the group to join hands and model the first prayer for the person on your right. Tell people they may either speak their prayer aloud or, if that makes anyone uncomfortable, pray in silence and then squeeze their neighbor's hand to indicate that prayer has been offered. If the group is larger than six people, form two groups and ask someone who is comfortable with the model to facilitate a second group.

At the end of the *lectio divina* segment you may ask the group members how they reacted to the model and then move on to some discussion of chapter 3. Questions you might ask include these: What vital rhythm for a life of faith and service are you living or trying to live? What factors in your life make such a rhythm difficult to sustain? Where have you found places of refreshment—the green pastures, and still waters of Psalm 23—in which you experience God restoring your soul?

Writing (20 minutes)
The last part of the evening is as before: Give people time for psalm writing.

Closing (10 minutes)
Conclude with a reminder of the next reading assignment and an invitation to participants to read their psalms.

Weeks 3 through 8

Now THAT YOU HAVE ESTABLISHED a basic structure, feel free to tweak the sessions in ways that help your group to pray the Psalms. Some people may still be uncomfortable with silence, so reassure them that even seasoned monks have to work at keeping still before God in order to listen. Gradually increase the time you give to silence. Encourage participants to practice being still and listening during their own prayer times at home. You can find chants in *The Upper Room Worshipbook* and other sources. You may wish to use recorded music of monastic chant as an alternative. Here are questions you might offer to participants each week:

Week 3 (based on chapter 4, Finding Stability in God's Faithfulness)
• When have you experienced God as your Rock?
• What do you do when the ground seems slippery on your spiritual journey?

Week 4 (based on chapter 5, Dealing with Disappointment. . . .)
• For what are you waiting?
• What difficult experiences have caused you to cry out in prayer, "How long, O LORD?"
• When have you felt forgotten by God? angry at God?

• When have you sensed that you were waiting *with* God in trust?

Week 5 (based on chapter 6, Celebrating Creation)
• What has the natural world taught you about God the Creator?
• When has time spent in nature led you to a sense of wonder?
• How are you caring for the Creation?

Week 6 (based on chapter 7, Touching the Holy in the Ordinary)
• Where have you seen God's presence or challenge in the ordinary things or events of your life?
• In what areas of your life are you seeking to widen the borders of inclusion and acceptance?

Week 7 (based on chapter 8, Discovering and Learning to Praise)
• When have you experienced praise of God as liberating and transformative?
• For what gifts from God are you especially grateful?
• How do you express this gratitude? What brings you joy?

Week 8 (based on rereading chapter 1, Hearing God's Word....)
• How has this group study changed the way you perceive the Psalms?
• In what ways have you found your voice by praying the Psalms and writing your own?
• Which psalm now best expresses your awareness of God in your life and in the life of the world?

Encourage Creativity

BE OPEN TO NEW IDEAS that emerge. For example, there may be interest in creating a group psalm book or in taking the opportunity to share some of the created psalms with a congregation or other gathering.

Whether you use this book alone or with others, its purpose is to help you live with the Psalms in such a way that they nourish, challenge, support, and strengthen you on your journey ever deeper into faith. The God our ancestors in the Hebrew tradition addressed still lives today and has expanded our experience of grace through Jesus, the Word made flesh. It is our joy to walk with Christ on the path of discipleship and to allow these ancient songs to accompany us along the way.